UNSTICK YOUR STUCK

How to Find Your Passion, Gain Clarity, and Play Bigger in Your Life

MELISSA S. MORRISON

NEW YORK

LONDON • NASHVILLE • MELBOURNE • VANCOUVER

UNSTICK YOUR STUCK

Published in New York, New York, by Morgan James Publishing in partnership with Difference Press.
www.MorganJamesPublishing.com

The Morgan James Speakers Group can bring authors to your live event. For more information or to book an event visit The Morgan James Speakers Group at
www.TheMorganJamesSpeakersGroup.com.

ISBN 978-1-68350-735-2 paperback
ISBN 978-1-68350-736-9 eBook
Library of Congress Control Number: 2017913175

Interior Design by:
Megan Whitney
Creative Ninja Designs
megan@creativeninjadesigns.com

In an effort to support local communities, raise awareness and funds, Morgan James Publishing donates a percentage of all book sales for the life of each book to Habitat for Humanity Peninsula and Greater Williamsburg.

Get involved today! Visit
www.MorganJamesBuilds.com

For All Survivors. Never give up on healing.
Your strength and courage will get you farther
than you can imagine. Trust in yourself.

CONTENT

INTRODUCTION

"There are two paths of which one may choose in the walk of life; one we are born with, and the one we consciously blaze. One is naturally true, while the other is a perceptive illusion. Choose wisely at each fork in the road."

T.F. HODGE, From Within I Rise: Spiritual Triumph over Death and Conscious Encounters with "The Divine Presence"

We all go through life-changing events, both expected and unexpected. The steps that we take after they occur can shape the way our future unfolds.

You have all heard the saying, "Three strikes and you're out." For me, it was four strikes and you're out. At least that's what I thought after the fourth time I was hit in the head with a softball. I had a concussion with so many debilitating symptoms that I never thought I would return to my everyday life. Now, my new normal is different than I expected, but I am doing what I love. Through it all, I found my love for life coaching and neuroscience.

April 17, 2012, was the night when my life changed in an instant. During a softball game, a ball tipped off my glove and hit me right between my eyes. My bell got rung – bad! I did not lose consciousness, but I was foggy and started experiencing dizziness and vision difficulties. The next morning, I went to work as an auditor at a CPA firm even though my head was pounding, my fatigue was unbearable, everything was foggy, lights and sounds were causing excruciating pain, my balance was so off I was walking into walls, and I had a hard time putting words together in a sentence, among other things. Yes, all those symptoms were happening to me at once.

It seems obvious now that I should have gone to the hospital right away, but at the time, I thought I could push through the symptoms. That morning, a co-worker stopped by my desk. "Good morning, Melissa. How are you doing today?"

"Oh my God!" I said as I covered my ears. "Why are you screaming at me?!" That was the moment I consciously realized something was significantly wrong.

A couple of my bosses came over to me to see how I was doing. "Melissa, what happened? Are you doing ok?"

"I was ... hit in the head ... last night ... with a softball. My head is ... hurting. I feel ... really out of it." I tried to explain to them what happened, but my sentences were in broken English. I was having a hard time speaking in complete sentences and trying to come up with the right words. What was happening to me?

My boss sent me home to rest. It wasn't until I stopped at the pharmacy on my way home from work that the pharmacist told me to go straight to the hospital. The hospital did an MRI and a CT scan of my brain. The doctor diagnosed me with a concussion, then sent me home. Alone. Now what?

Nobody talked to me about the long-term effects of a traumatic brain injury (TBI), but from that day, I felt I was facing an uphill battle, not only with the pain and disorientation from the injury itself, but also in trying to live a normal life. I was having a hard time accepting my new limitations. I didn't want to accept all the changes that come with a TBI: cognitive impairments, sensitivity to sound and light, short-term memory loss, and horrific headaches, to name a few. I just wanted the old me back and to feel better.

I tried to work part-time from home – from my bed, even – for the first couple of months after my injury. It was very hard working in the condition I was in. My head was pounding around the clock, and my fatigue so strong I needed to sleep many hours a day. My doctor eventually put me on medical leave. My new full-time job was going to doctors' appointments and occupational, speech, and physical therapies three times a week.

As a result of post-concussion syndrome, which is defined by symptoms that persist for months or years after a concussion, I was unable to continue working at the CPA firm, even after trying to go back to work many times. They finally let me go in December 2012, eight months after my injury. Suddenly I was out of a job, knee-deep in post-concussion symptoms, and had no clue where to go from there.

It was undeniably hard, but I realized as time went on that my injury and being let go was a blessing in disguise. This was the wake-up call that I had always wanted and needed. I hadn't enjoyed the work I'd been doing as an auditor, and I'd even told my boss at the end of the previous year that I hated my job. I knew I was meant to do more in my life and wanted to do something where I felt more of service to others. I had no idea what that was, though, at the time. Being unemployed while trying to heal from the concussion turned out to be the perfect opportunity for me to figure it out. I enrolled in a women's leadership program and discovered that I wanted to become a life coach. I became a certified coach about a year and a half later and never looked back.

You might be wondering why my last concussion is relevant here. I told you my story because that final concussion, by far the worst of several, marked a pivotal point in my life and pushed me to go after the life that I want and deserve. To live a more fulfilled life. That was the day I received my wake-up call from the universe. Getting hit in the head has a way of making you stop your life in your tracks. For me, it apparently took getting hit in the head with a softball four times to make me stop my life in my tracks.

I wanted to write this book so I could prevent other people from getting hit in the head. Probably even literally. I had my bell rung for you! Just take that in. I took the hit in the head and took on a bigger role so I can help you soar in your life. You are an amazing person and deserve all of the happiness and fulfillment in your life and heart, like I do, like we all do.

Just take that in! We go through our day-to-day lives on autopilot. We get up each morning at about the same time, get ready, sit in traffic, go to work, get our to-do list done, maybe play on the Internet for a bit when the boss isn't watching, talk to co-workers, go to meetings, then come home to make dinner and go to bed. We do the same thing over and over again five days a week and, if we are lucky, we get the weekend off. Do you want something different to happen in there? Some excitement that mixes up the mundane? Something to unstick the stuckness?

What if I told you that I will jump on this ride with you to find what you want out of your life and help you get it?! I want to be there with you to see it through. It won't be easy. There will be times when you will want to quit, but I won't let you if this is something that you truly want. Anyone can stay unfulfilled and stuck in their life. I know, because I did it for 10 years. If I would have had someone say they would be there along with me, I would've jumped on it. This book will provide you with the steps you need to determine the passions you have in life, gain clarity on your next steps, and learn how to take the jump to soar.

CHAPTER 1
CURRENT STATUS: UNFULFILLED

"To live a life that is wrong for you is a form of dying. There are people who have lives that look perfect. They try to be happy, they believe they should be happy, they are trying to like it, but if it's off course from their north star, they aren't satisfied."

MARTHA BECK

Your current status in life is feeling unfulfilled. You feel it every day when you wake up in the morning and look in the mirror. There is a part of you missing. On the outside it looks like you have it made. You may have a great family and a great set of friends. You graduated with a bachelor's or master's degree from a respectable university. You have a job that anyone would tell you is amazing, and you have achieved accomplishments that put you higher in the field of work you are in. *But,* and it's a big *but,* a piece of *you* is missing. You have a hole in you that you don't know how to fill. There are parts of you that you aren't even sure you want to fill because you don't know what changes that may bring to your life.

Feeling like a Fraud

It's hard because you work at a job that pays good money. Why change a good thing, right? But deep down, you know that there's a problem, and hiding it makes you feel like a fraud.

In a sense, I believe we all feel like frauds in some ways in our lives. Maybe it is with our jobs. We excel at our work and get to work on time each day. We give our all and contribute in meetings when we are supposed to, but the work that we do is not what we were called to do or meant to do in our lives. We are undercover frauds. Sometimes it's obvious that someone isn't meant to do the work. Bob may show up late every day for his job and never put in the time to complete his tasks. Sally's undercover fraudulence reveals itself when all she talks about is her love for animals and taking care of them when they are sick and wishing she was a veterinarian – but she still completes her accounting reports on time. Other times it might just be you coming into work every day, doing what you are assigned to do because you are supposed to do it, punching the time card, getting paid, and going home. I don't know about you, but year after year of being an undercover fraud wore me out.

Another way we can feel like a fraud is in a relationship. You start dating someone because you like them. You have similar interests and you enjoy each other's company. Down the road, they may fall in love with you. You continue on, even though you wonder if this might not be the one for you. A little part of you feels like a fraud because you know this might not be the right person, but then again, maybe they are. Your heart is not fully in it, even though you know the other person's heart is fully in it. What do you do when that happens? Do you continue to stay in that relationship, or do you break it off?

We recognize when a hole is in our heart, whether that hole reveals itself at work or in a relationship. What makes us decide to stay anyway? Both are integral parts of our lives. When we are not at work, we are usually with the significant other.

Perhaps you feel like a fraud socially or financially. When others look at you and your family, they see dollar signs and diamonds. You roll up to soccer practice in your Cadillac Escalade. Friends and acquaintances see you mingling at a party with your designer handbag at your side and wearing your designer shoes. Then you go home for the evening to take care of the bills and realize that you don't have enough money in the bank account to pay for your mortgage. You are hit by a wave of feeling like an undercover fraud. You realize that you are in too deep, feeling like you need to prove to everyone on the outside that everything is perfect in your life and nothing negative is going on. That you aren't struggling just to get by every month. You don't want anyone to see that you aren't the polished veneer of a person that they see out in public. The thought that everyone might guess what is really going on behind closed doors and that you're in over your head is too scary. People might not want to talk to you anymore. It doesn't feel possible that they would accept you, and you could breathe easier knowing that you don't have to keep up this facade. You just don't know what to do. So there you are. Status: fraud.

In any of these three scenarios, how do we figure out what is best for us to do?

Our Brains Are Patterned Machines

We get to a certain point in our lives where we have a story that continuously runs in our heads. Yours might be: But I went to school and spent thousands and thousands of dollars to become an engineer, so that is what I am supposed to do. At least, that's what my client George told me when we began working together. He went to Penn State to become an electrical engineer. Once he graduated, he got a job, and, for the next 11 years, that was what he did. He wasn't happy, but he didn't know how to do it differently or what he wanted until our work together brought him new awareness of and belief in the fact that he was allowed to find a career that he was passionate about. That it was okay to go after it.

Growing up, we are taught that we go to school to get a degree in something, and then we go off and do that thing for the next 40 years or so. Our brains are patterned machines. As complex as our brain is, it is also simple. It likes having us do the same thing over and over again. It can predict what we are going to do before we even do it. Although this is extremely useful in most areas of our lives, it is also a hindrance, especially when it comes time to changing something up. You've probably noticed that you don't have to put much attention into your drive to work every day. You zone out, and then, the next thing you know, you're driving into the parking lot at work in the morning.

Experts say that it takes about 21 days, or up to two months, to break a habit. There are many variables that come into play that can make the number bigger or smaller, but that is the approximate amount. Just like in life, unless I know a new way that I want to go, I will probably stick with going the same route I do every day. In the equation of life, going the same route every day equals staying with that hole in my heart. Staying at the same job that is unfulfilling. After all, I did spend all of that money to go to school for it, right? And I'm good at it, so that counts for something, right?

Reasons for Staying Unfulfilled

Before we start changing our brains' patterns, I want to talk about the reasons why you are staying unfulfilled in your life. I know these reasons because I had the same ones running through my head at one point in my life as well. You might match up with some of them, or perhaps all of them. Either way, I want you to know that you are not alone.

One of the first questions that has stopped you in the past from taking the steps to fill that hole inside is: What if I can't figure out what I want to do? This is a normal question to ask when you don't know where to go next. So far, your life has been basically laid out for you since graduation from college. You knew what direction to go as far as your job path. You may not have known what company to work for or where in the country you wanted to live, but you knew what line of work to look for when in search of a job. Once you're in that field, you know whether you have to go back for your master's or doctorate to get ahead or whether you have to study to get a particular certification or license. It's not easy to go up to your boss and tell them that you might want to do something else for a living, but aren't sure what. Most of the time, they won't care. They just want your work done and completed on time to meet the deadlines.

Another reason stopping you is worrying that you'll pick the wrong thing. We have become a society that is afraid to fail or lose. Perhaps you always wanted to become a photographer, so you buy all of the equipment, start taking clients and doing photo shoots for weddings, and then *bam!* You realize that this is not something that you want to do at all. You aren't enjoying yourself like you once did when photography was just a hobby years ago. It sucks because you went ahead and spent tons of money on equipment and taking photography classes to learn the proper techniques to help you take amazing pictures. Wow, you feel like you wasted the money and time and now you are back to square one. Now what? Do you go back and do what you used to do and keep that hole growing inside of you? Let's jump back on the unfulfillment train because at least you'll be making good money again. Chugga. Chugga. Deep in the hole again.

The next reason that might be stopping you is the belief that you won't have the support to do what you want to do. Life can be a lonely journey at times, so when we have the support of our family and friends it can be a big boost. If you are working in a career – let's say accounting – that your parents supported and pushed you to work in back when determining what you were going to major in back in college, it's probable that there will be pushback when you go to them and say that now you want to become a chef. What a huge shift of the pendulum.

Your friends may feel the same. As I mentioned earlier, our brains are patterned machines. We don't like change and that includes change outside of ourselves. It will shift the paradigm. Uh-oh, Maria isn't going to be going to her office job anymore and I'm going to have to be there for her when she fails or succeeds. I've noticed that it happens a lot when it is geared more towards the unknown. If you want to get into a job field that your family or friends don't know much about, then there is more apprehension there. Also, the bigger the leap, the bigger the fear that comes with it for you and your support system.

Maybe you worry that you don't have the money to make a change. This can be a giant setback for people. After all, money is what makes the world go round – or so the saying goes. This is a valid reason that might be keeping you in a state of unfulfillment. Student loan debt or credit card debt could be holding you back. How much money do you really need to start taking those baby steps toward gaining clarity? We feel that money is the be-all, end-all, and that we need it to do anything differently in our lives. We can use it as a crutch to keep us in the same state of being.

Perhaps your reason is fear of risk. Being able to acknowledge that you feel this way is already a huge step in the right direction. There is a risk in almost anything you do in life. Getting in your car every day and driving is a risk; you are risking that you will get into an accident, whether it would be your fault or the fault of another driver. Asking a person out on a date is a risk. You risk the chance of getting rejected and having the person say no. In the same instance though, you are risking the chance of the person saying yes and therefore you finding happiness with that one person to love and spend your life with. What a great risk/reward balance! The same effort you are putting into being afraid to take the risk is the same, if not more, of a reward that you would get out of it by finding that passion that will fill that hole that is deepening inside of you.

The final reason you might hesitate to take a chance on change: What if you succeed at it? Some people may look at this question and wonder why I put it there. I believe that with certain things in life, we can have a fear of failure and/or a fear of success. The more vulnerable you are, the more fear of succeeding comes about. Think about it. You will be seen and unable to hide when you are doing something that you are truly passionate about. When you start soaring in your life and flying, it is for all to see. Not everyone feels built to withstand that attention. That is why many of us continue to go through life with that hole inside of us. We dare ourselves to play small, living a life of mediocrity. We wear a mask to hide behind who we are meant to be.

Someday Is Not a Day of the Week

I want to share a quote with you that one of my best friends and I still say to this day, "Someday is not a day of the week." I first learned about it back in college. I printed it out and hung it on my wall in my dorm room. I still have that print-out to this day. This quote stuck out to me because so many times when we are talking about wanting to do more with our lives, we say, "I'll do it someday." Just like the quote, someday is not a day of the week. When we don't put a timeline on our goals, then they will rarely get completed. If I stated that someday I'll write this book, two years from now I would probably still be saying that I'm going to write it. I turned my 'someday' into 'now' by bringing the right people into my life to get me the result I wanted since I wasn't able to do it on my own. I hired a book coach to help keep me on track, recognize the author in me, and help me stay accountable in my writing. During your journey I'd love for you to go online and find the quote "Someday is not a day of the week" and print it out. Keep it in front of you as a reminder that nothing will get accomplished and filled within you if you don't put your heart into it and have an achievement date in mind.

When we are feeling stuck and unfulfilled every day, it begins to really weigh heavily on our hearts and in our heads. It changes who we are inside and out. We might feel like a shell of the person we used to be at some point in our lives. There are valid reasons as to why you are in the stuck status. I know, because I have personally felt every single one of them. Knowing that someday is not a day of the week, I am curious: Why haven't you started on your journey to figure out your dream yet? It is ok if you are scared and don't know what the path is moving forward. We will get you there. It takes time and effort, and I will be right there with you as you take those steps.

CHAPTER 2

I'VE BEEN THERE, HOLE AND ALL

"My mission in life is not merely to survive,
but to thrive; and to do so with some passion, some
compassion, some humor, and some style."

MAYA ANGELOU

f only we had a crystal ball to go back and change things in the past to go down another path. I had a hole in me the size of Texas. My life sucked, or at least I felt like it did on the inside. That hole was debilitating. I dreaded going into work most days. I didn't care about the work. Deep down I knew working at a CPA firm as an auditor wasn't what I wanted to spend my life doing.

My College Path

I majored in accounting in college. How are we supposed to know at age 18 what we want to do when we grow up? I was

17

good at math in school, and my parents thought it would be a good route to major in accounting, so I did it. My dad majored in accounting and has his own business. I always thought it would be cool to have my own business one day, so I went for it.

I started out interested in psychology. I wanted to declare it as my major, but I didn't. I wanted to help others. I was always reading self-help books to better myself, and psychology seemed like the perfect field for me to go into. That's when my parents stepped in. All I heard from them is that you don't make any money working in that field unless you go on to get your doctorate. I couldn't imagine myself being in school for most of my 20s after spending so much time already in school, and going to get a doctorate sounded hard. I got good grades in school, but I didn't want to be in school forever. So I majored in accounting. I mean, I was good at math, and my parents knew better than I did at that time in my life, so it must have been right. Right?

Back to that hole in me. Would I even have this hole in me if I went to school for what I originally wanted to do? I don't know. All I knew was that I didn't like what I was doing. There was a piece missing in me.

My Career Path

I worked as an auditor straight out of college for the U.S. Navy. I wasn't crunching numbers, so it wasn't too bad. The majority of the audits were not the same, so it mixed things up. I wasn't totally bored, just unfulfilled. We got to travel around the country as well. That was a definite perk, but it still wasn't enough, so after four and a half years I went for something a little different and got a job as a business consultant. In my head, I thought I could keep moving around trying different things in the business arena until, hopefully, the fulfillment would come.

That second job lasted a year. My unhappiness was bleeding into other parts of my life, including my love relationships. That is when I took things into my own hands, quit my job, and asked my best friend from college to join me on a two-month journey backpacking in Egypt and then around most of Western Europe. It was the first thing I had done in a long time that was fulfilling. During my backpacking trip, it felt like I was soaring in life, taking life by the horns and enjoying it. I thought I would be able to take this newfound fulfillment back with me to the States and use it when I returned. That did *not* happen. Instead, the economy crashed – it was 2008 – and no one was hiring. My plan collapsed in on me. I eventually had to move back down to the Washington D.C. area and landed a job at a CPA firm. Doing auditing. Again.

Stuck in Fraud Status

I love watching crime shows, especially those true crime series where they are able to solve a case based on forensic evidence. They catch the murderer because a piece of carpet fiber from his car was found at the victim's house after it fell off his shoe. Fighting fraud using forensics is also very pertinent in the business world. A forensic accountant looks through the accounting records of a company looking for fraud. They might find a fictitious subcontractor, for instance, providing fake services to the company under investigation. Then they might see that an employee is writing checks from the company to this fictitious subcontractor, drawn from a bank account set up in the employee's name. Gotcha! The bad guy gets caught!

I thought I was going to solve my problem of the unfulfillment hole that had returned since being back working as an auditor by studying to become a Certified Fraud Examiner (CFE). I studied and passed my test to become certified a few months later.

It was ironic. I was a Certified Fraud Examiner, and yet in my real life I still felt like a fraud. There I was, coming into work every day at a job that I didn't particularly care for and wishing I was doing something else entirely. The problem was, I had no idea what else I wanted to do, so I felt like I was stuck in fraud status. How many frauds do you have around you at work? So many of us work at jobs that we don't care to be doing, but we still get the job done.

There was pain being stuck in that place. A pressure in my chest that made it hard to breathe another breath. But I still went on. Looking in the mirror it was like I could see the hole in my heart through my chest. What was it going to take to change this feeling going on inside of me?

It's like when we get a cut. Our bodies heal by creating a scab, but if we pick at it, it will bleed again. What makes us keep picking at the scab? What would happen if we just let it bleed? Let the feelings flow out of us? As the blood drips down our leg and onto the ground it leaves a trace of us wherever we are. Leaving that trace of me is what I was looking for in my life.

To leave a lasting impression with whomever I came in contact with. But there I was ... a fraud living each day with a mask on to protect the person inside and just going through the motions of everyday life.

Disappointing the Family

After all, my family was so proud of me. I had the guts to move out of state, away from all of my family. I lived in big ol' Washington D.C. I was now a CFE and working at a CPA firm. I was making really good money. They would tease me that I would be the one to buy the vacation house for the family to use. It really came down to me not wanting to disappoint my family. I didn't want to become the failure in the family when it felt like they held me in such high regard. I would just stick it out, and maybe I would eventually find my way into fulfillment.

Always for the Money

I didn't know what I wanted to do for a career, but the money I was making as an auditor was a big obstacle for me to get over in wanting to try something else. I didn't know how to figure it out without quitting my job and trying new things until I found that *thing* that lit me up inside. I couldn't take that chance with the money I was making. I tried to volunteer at the hospital and other places around the city to see if it sparked anything inside. I could help people on the side, but keep my main job as an auditor. What I didn't know at the time was that I was meant to be of service to other people as a full-time job, not just in my spare time.

Red Flag – CPA Test: Audit Section

One red flag that I should have recognized at the time was when I was studying for my CPA test. If I wanted to keep moving up in the company, I had to get my CPA license. That was one of the things I had on my bucket list to obtain. Exciting bucket list, right? Ha! I studied for it while I was working. There are four parts to the CPA test: Business Concepts, Regulation, Audit, and Financial Accounting and Reporting. I passed the Business Concepts and Regulation sections on the first try. That is something that doesn't happen very often. On the other hand, I *failed* Audit three times! Yes, you read that correctly. I failed the Audit section of the test three times. I had worked as an auditor for most of my career, yet I could not pass that section of the exam. Looking back, it's obvious the universe was trying to tell me something. I can laugh now about it. I thought that it was going to be a slam-dunk. Nope. I was wrong.

Foreshadowing

It was the end of the year prior to my brain injury, and I was in my boss's office going over the year in review. I had been working on litigation efforts in the office for part of the year, and I'd enjoyed it. I wanted to do more of it, but my boss told me that they needed me back to work at an audit with a client I had worked with for the previous couple years. She knew that it wasn't what I wanted; I had told her that I hated auditing. Who in their right mind tells their boss that they hate their job? This girl right here. I knew it wouldn't change anything because

I would still leave her office and put the same amount of effort into the work as I had before. Only this time I could feel that the hole in me was getting bigger, and I didn't know how much longer I was going to be able to hang on.

My Wake-up Call

The timing of my brain injury was very ironic. We were about a week away from the entrance conference to start the audit that I was told I had to work on again. I played softball in a recreational league in Virginia, where I was living at the time. I was playing first base in the game with a runner on first. The batter hit the ball, and a player from my team threw it to second base to get the front runner out. There was no longer a play at first base to get a double play because the runner already touched first base and ran through the base into the outfield, but the player that caught the ball on second base threw the ball to me anyway. I did not expect them to throw the ball with no play, but I did see the ball coming at the last second. There was enough time to put my glove up and stop the ball from hitting me full force, but it tipped off of my glove and hit me right between the eyes. When someone says that they got their bell rung, I now understand what they mean. I got my bell rung. It was the wake-up call that I needed. The instant the ball hit me between the eyes, it changed my life forever.

I didn't have a choice about needing time to heal from my brain injury, but I did have a choice about how I was going to react and what I was going to do with myself while I was healing. Since I couldn't go back to work – my doctors and my employer stopped me several times after I tried to return – I chose to take advantage of the time I'd been given. Besides healing my head from my injury, I knew it was time to heal the hole in my heart as well. It felt like I'd been given a present, and it was my choice whether I wanted to make it the best gift that I had ever received.

My New Path Forward

I had been to a couple of women's empowerment conferences, one right before my injury and one the year previous. I knew there were people out there to help others figure out what their next path should be. I didn't realize at the time that I would eventually blossom into one of those coaches that I was seeking out after my injury occurred. I found a women's leadership program led by Tara Mohr called Playing Big. She works with women to find their voice and helps them bring it out in their work and in their lives. This was a critical piece in my journey: finding a program led by a life coach to help me determine what path I want to take next. During the work of the program, I resolved that my path was to become a life coach myself. To help others who were stuck and help them move forward. If I had not had this wake-up call in the form of getting hit in the head by a softball – for the FOURTH time – I don't believe that I would have found this path. Or if I had, it would have taken me many more years to come to it.

One part of the program was going out to try our calling and gain feedback. I found my first coaching clients, and I found that I loved working with them. Seeing the shifts in people, helping them get unstuck from whatever was stopping them from moving forward, was very rewarding. In those short weeks of working with the clients, I felt a kind of joy and fulfillment I never knew in all of my years working in accounting. I finally found what I wanted to do and how I wanted to spend my days: being able to provide a mirror for others and being alongside them as they grew and became more authentic in their lives. I had to figure out how to get started right away. My brain injury wasn't going to stop me from getting certified so I could go out and work with more people.

Doing the research to find out where the elite coaches who I admired had gotten certified took me to the Coaches Training Institute. I signed up, and classes started a few months later. I found my people. The energy in those classes was like nothing I had ever felt before. I was eating it up, and my hunger kept growing. This was what life was all about. I took the classes, and went through CTI's certification process. I got certified a year to the day after I started the certification process. I never would've imagined I could get through the program with how I was feeling at the time. My symptoms were still there, but when a fire is lit inside us, anything is possible. That is what I truly believe, especially now looking back at all I have gone through.

My Love for Neuroscience

A leader of one of my coaching classes was the expert in neuroscience for the Coaches Training Institute. At that time, I was starting to do more research on the neuroscience of the brain to help myself heal. There is only so much that doctors are able to do to help the patients. A lot of it is up to the patients themselves. That is the same elsewhere in life; you can lead a horse to water, but you can't make it drink. I introduced myself to the neuroscience guru and resolved to learn all I could from her. I fell in love with neuroscience that day. I knew it was something else I had to add to my toolbox to not only help myself, but also help others. I hired her as my coach so I could learn as much as I could from her and to have her push me as much as she could by using neuroscientific principles so I could learn firsthand the power of our brains.

After I got certified as a coach, I started taking classes in neuroscience and coaching. It is fascinating how our brain functions and what it is able to do if we can use it in the right way, to our advantage. We have the power to heal ourselves. Our brains continue to grow and change due to their neuroplasticity. This concept has been my friend ever since I learned it, and it helped make me into the person that I am today. The more I learned about the brain and neuroscience, the more I healed from my brain injury. It also helped me be more in service to my clients. Many people– especially the former me, being very far left-brained– love having scientific evidence to understand why we act and do certain things. This was the perfect solution for those people. I was able to explain to them why our brains work this way, and help them see that we can trick our own brains into working in different ways to help us move forward in our journeys. What power neuroscience can bring to our lives! I had to keep learning.

My passion and fulfillment just kept growing and growing. I continued to have this hunger. I started doing research on nutrition, meditation, and the power of storytelling, as well as neuroscience. I came across a modality called Neurosculpting®. It was like it fell right into my lap. It combined all of them into one. How lucky was I? I started to take classes and noticed the power they held. My healing for my brain injury accelerated more than it had in the past year. I was at a plateau in my healing, and this helped tremendously. I knew I had to bring this modality to others. I continued to take classes and went on to become a Certified Neurosculpting® Facilitator. I would be able to bring this healing modality using meditation to help with our overall health. How powerful could this get? I was very excited.

The Possibilities Ahead

Now, thinking back just a few years to where I was with that hole inside of me, I see that I was living my own hell, one that not many people knew about. I wasn't enjoying what I was doing. It's a huge contrast to now, when I am at a place where I cannot get enough of what I am learning each day and the services that I am able to provide others in my coaching and Neurosculpting® classes and sessions. If someone had asked me right after my injury if I would be at this point in five years, I would have thought they were nuts.

I want you to find the same purpose and joy. I can tell you that it is possible. I want to be there to see the shift in your life and bring the clarity that you need to play bigger. My book is something simple to take you forward, too.

I have to be honest with you. Total transparency here. I never wanted to be a writer. I sucked at writing, or I thought I did. I got a C in college in English class. I never thought I was creative. It wasn't until I started writing blog posts that other people started telling me how well I wrote and that they loved reading my work. It took me probably six months or so to finally own the title of "writer." It felt weird. You will feel the same way with whatever aspects of yourself you find through the process of reading my book. You might not want to own whatever comes up at first, to accept that this is what you could do with your life. It might be a dream that you always wanted, but never thought would happen or ever even could be. That is perfectly normal. I never thought that I would become a coach or fall in love with neuroscience. You are one foot from the edge, and I want to help you take the next step to soar. You will never know what you are capable of being or doing unless you trust the process. What do you have to lose?

When my client Linda started working with me, she was cautious about what she would be able to achieve. She had worked as a pre-school teacher for most of her career. She had other passions, but never thought anything would develop from them. At our first session, she told me that she was hesitant about the process.

I reminded Linda that this was normal. Our brains are used to doing the same things every day, and when we begin to change things up, there will be some resistance. I asked her to trust me and trust the process, because it has worked many times with other clients.

As we worked together, Linda explored her passion for planning parties and helping friends get things set up for their weddings. She noticed that while planning her friend's 40th birthday party, a joy came over her as she was making sure the cake was done and would arrive at the right time, and that the venue was ready and the proper amount of food was ordered and prepared. She asked her friend if she could take the lead in making sure that the party was on budget and that all of the planning was taken care of. It turned out to be her first steps on the path to becoming a very happy event planner.

I want to help you take the next step to soar because I know the feeling of waking up every morning and having something missing from your life. I know what it feels like to have that hole inside you that only you can see when you look into the mirror each day. Feeling numb going into work every day, doing the same thing over and over again with no sense of gratitude as you walk out the door at the end of the day. That stuckness that you feel, like you are walking through tar and you can't shake it off your shoes. No matter what you do, it's there. What kind of life is that to lead? It feels like you are in a tunnel with no light at the end. If you are reading this book, then you are already starting on the bridge to cross over to the land of fulfillment. I want to be alongside you as you walk over the bridge. I will not let the bridge collapse underneath you.

CHAPTER 3
S.O.A.R.I.N.G.

"In order to fly, you're going to have to let go of the world that you're hanging onto."

KUREK ASHLEY

When I first started out on my journey, after my brain injury, I was very lost. I didn't know if I would be able to find what I wanted to spend the rest of my life doing. I had spent so much time and money already going to school for accounting and working in the accounting world that I didn't know if I would be able to figure it out. It felt like I was going to stay in the same status forever. Stuck. I'm sure you are feeling similar to how I felt. In our everyday life, it is very easy for us to change our focus to do a different task, but to actually change our mindset and the way our brain works as a patterned machine is a different story. It gets old looking at ourselves in the mirror each day and seeing that hole inside of us. It's like being grounded on earth with your wings stuck together. It's time to unstick your wings.

This framework that you are about to embark on learning and undertaking will not only help you sew up the hole inside of you, it will also give you the ability to soar in your life. I call this process S.O.A.R.I.N.G., and we'll look at each step in the following chapters. You can use this process to get you unstuck from where you are currently to find what you are passionate about and transform your life moving forward and playing bigger. In the S.O.A.R.I.N.G. process, you will take your life off of auto-pilot to create lasting change.

S – Setting the Stage

Before implementing anything, the stage has to be set. It helps to get you in the right mindset to imagine a greater space for you to fill in the world. Creating an intention and embodying a new being helps to set the stage. It brings your mind, body, and soul into alignment for the journey ahead. Then you will be writing "I Am" statements to aid in realizing that you have all you need already in you for the journey.

O – On the Hunt for Passions and Values

You will begin to realize the parts of you that you want to highlight and ignite within. Pivotal moments in your life can be key in identifying where your path should take you. Being able to understand and recognize what drives you and brings out your passionate side helps steer you in the right direction. The values that we hold in our lives are a piece of our inner compass that we should pay attention to. You will be identifying what values are present and missing from your life. Making a list of what you are passionate about will get your wheels turning and help in the process of becoming unstuck. You'll see that other paths are available to you that ignite you within.

A – Attaining Clarity

Awareness and clarity will be revealed to you in this chapter. You will begin to have a relationship with your passions, getting to know them like you would a friend. You will take a look at your old limiting beliefs that have held you back in the past and learn to look at them in a different, more functional way. To move forward in a more resourceful way, you will give yourself permission to let go of the things in your life that are holding you back. Lastly, in this step you will do a visualization that will help you clear the fog and direct you on the path ahead.

R – Ready for the Leap

A new path is ahead, and you will begin to see a new awareness to fill the hole that you feel inside. You will pinpoint targets that you want to attain to further narrow down your passions. Then you'll take your first step by doing what I call leaping. A leap is like planting little seedlings into the ground and seeing which one will grow to become a strong tree.

I – Inner and Outer Critic

In this process of bringing to life your passions, it is natural to expect the inner and outer critics to pop up. You will learn to recognize inner and outer critics when they arise and how to manage them. You will understand how to personify the inner critic, therefore helping it lose its power. We'll talk about the role of the outer critic, and why it is always more about them than it is about you.

N – New Foundation to Build

In starting anything new, it is best to begin by building a strong foundation. The stronger the foundation, the more it can withstand when obstacles arise. In this chapter, you will make a commitment to yourself on your new journey by beginning to build a foundation. Building a foundation is like a tree having good and strong roots to grow and flourish. You will create a new intention going forward and say yes to make a commitment to the process of making your passion a reality. You will learn that surrounding yourself with people that embody what you want to bring into your life will benefit you in moving forward and achieving your goals.

G – Getting into Action

In this chapter, you will take the lead in this new creation of yourself and take action. To take action, you will identify small steps to help you move forward and establish deadlines to get you moving immediately. I will discuss the reasons for having an accountability partner during this process. Recognizing resources that you already have available to you will also help you in being able to move forward as soon as possible.

All of this may seem like a lot of work to do. I was completely overwhelmed when I started on my journey after my brain injury, because I had no idea which way to go or if I would ever figure out what I wanted to do. But I designed this process to make your journey easier. I use what I learned about neuroscience and our brains to take an integrated approach, using both your left and right sides of your brain, which increases the likelihood of creating lasting change. We need to change the patterns that our brains have set. If I was able to go through the process of changing the patterns in my brain to create lasting change and find my passion in life, I promise you that you will be able to as well. That is one of the benefits of having a plastic brain, it gives us the ability to grow and change. Our brains are set up to help us succeed when using the proper processes.

The tools and exercises in the S.O.A.R.I.N.G. process have helped me and my clients navigate the waters, gain clarity, and move forward and out of the unfulfilled and stuck status. You will be a different person at the end of this process. Buckle up and get ready to unstick your stuck.

CHAPTER 4
SETTING THE STAGE

"The nature of the cosmos is such that whatever vision you have about yourself and the world will become reality."

ALBERTO VILLODO

I believe when we are starting any new endeavor that we need to set our environment up to be open and receive what is waiting for us. We will be going through multiple tools to help us set up the stage for this journey. We will be writing an intention to help plant the seed at the beginning of our journey to start to imagine a bigger space for you to fill in the world. Then we will be writing I Am statements to see what we are already equipped with before setting off on this journey together.

One of the first questions I believe you should ask before starting on a new journey is: Do you want this? Are you ready to begin on this journey to gain clarity and find something you are passionate about and to play bigger in your life? This might sound like a silly question, but until you make up your mind to commit on this journey to whatever may unfold, then we won't get very far. Do you want to quit going into work every day with that hole inside of you? Do you want to stop using any of the valid excuses that are holding you back from getting started? Do you want this, whatever this may end up being? Yes? Then let's do it. Commit to this and see what unfolds. You may surprise yourself.

Setting an Intention

The next thing that I feel it is good to do when doing anything, especially anything new, is setting an intention. I believe that it is the starting point to get our mind, body, spirit, and the universe in line with each other. The dictionary defines intention as "an act or instance of determining mentally upon some action or result." I like the way the dictionary defines intention: the act of determining mentally. If we don't put what we want out there, then the chance of it coming into realization diminishes. I believe that when we set intentions, we use our time and energy more wisely and put them toward what we are wanting. I like the way Deepak Chopra talks about intentions: "Intentions are the triggers for transformation in the body. If you want to wiggle your toes, you do it through intention."

Setting an intention plants a seed that you will tend and water as we embark on this journey. Once we plant these seeds in our subconscious, they can begin to grow and flourish. I prefer to create intentions during quiet, relaxing times in my day, whether it be first thing in the morning when I wake up, or later, at a time of day when I don't have a million things going on at once. So I would love for you to go to a quiet place when you are writing your intention. Grab a notebook and a pen and write it down. Writing it down is key because you can read it when you feel the need and it can be a reminder for you. I want you to take about five minutes and just marinate on the question: *What is your intention for this journey?* This does not have to be a concrete answer. At this point, we have no idea what the result might be. Just focus on the mindset that you want to have, or a general idea of a bigger picture.

One example of an intention might be to allow yourself to be open to the process of gaining clarity on your next steps. Another example of an intention might be to give yourself permission to let go and fully embark on the process. Your intention can be as simple as intending for everything to happen as it will and being open to let the opportunities come through you. There is no wrong way to set an intention. This is something for you to be able to put out into the universe to free yourself up for this process. To be able to think about all of the possibilities that may come about as we are going along through the journey, whether expected or unexpected. What do you want for yourself?

Embodying Your Intention

After you write your intention down, take a moment to close your eyes and embody the new presence being created. Think of the person that you want to become in this process. Imagine the intention that you just set in place and focus your thoughts on bringing it into fruition. Draw in the intention as you breathe five deep breaths. Allow it to fill each of the crevices of your body and all of the spaces. What does it feel like to have this intention created in you? As you are breathing out, imagine breathing out this old unfulfilled piece of you. You may be able to breathe out pieces of it right now, or maybe not yet. Don't judge it. Just notice what is happening in your body. Now, if it feels right, take note of what is going on in your body and in your mind. What thoughts are you having right now?

To help further your envisioning, I invite you to create a drawing, a vision board, or a collage to help you in setting your intention to plant the seed. I personally love doing vision boards. It helps me to get my focus on what I am wanting in my life. I take a piece of poster board and go through old magazines and even advertisements that I receive in the mail to see what stands out to me. I use this to even further propel my thinking of what will happen in the future. It doesn't have to be physical items that you find, it can be quotes or sayings. Maybe you see the word "love" in a magazine. You can rip that out and put it on the poster board. It can help you keep in mind that you want to embody more love for yourself during this process. You might also want to cut out pictures of people or things that embody what you want to be represented more fully in your life. Maybe it's a group of people sitting at a table conversing, and they are all laughing and smiling. This could represent many things to you, but what comes to mind for me is to bring more fun and laughter into your life. Maybe more camaraderie. The possibilities are endless when it comes to what you can put on a vision board. This process will begin to set you up to imagine what is possible to bring into your life or heighten what is already in your life.

My client Jim enjoyed working as a life coach, but was having a hard time with motivation and how to grow his business. He was stuck. This was causing him a lot of havoc and affecting other parts of his life. He noticed that he wasn't trying to go out to get more clients, and, in his personal life, bumps in his relationship with his girlfriend were starting to come up on the path. He was allowing a lot of outside noise to get in his way, and it was beginning to cripple him. I had him do this last exercise, wanting him to get grounded again on his intention for what he was doing and how he wanted to serve his clients and himself. I knew it would help him get his focus back on what was important and what he wanted to get from our time working together. This was a crucial and a key exercise for him.

His intention was to allow himself to be more open and learn how to trust his inner voice again. He felt like he had veered off course and wanted to get back on again. During one of our phone sessions, I asked Jim to describe to me what going off course and wanting to get back on again felt like to him.

He said, "Melissa, it feels like I am a small fishing boat out in the middle of the ocean, and the waves are crashing into my boat. I am getting knocked around back and forth. Water is splashing in the sides of my boat. I don't have control over the boat, and I'm starting to sink."

Then he stopped right in his tracks and got quiet.

"Jim? Are you still there?" I asked.

"Yes, I am," Jim replied. "I just realized that to withstand the waves out in the ocean, I need to be a sturdier boat. I want to be one of those old, wooden pirate ships that you see in old movies. I want my ship to have sails strong enough to carry me through the windy seas. That is how I can get back on course."

"Yes! And what changed for you in that moment when you paused?" I asked him.

"I realized that I was the one in charge of what boat I was in while out in the ocean. By making one small shift of a change in the boat, it is a start on learning how to trust my inner voice again, or maybe even learning to have a better understanding in myself going forward in the process," Jim answered.

I then asked Jim what would be a way that he would be able to further sow the seed in himself to use going forward besides writing down his intention. I suggested to him that he could create a vision board or perhaps create a drawing.

"Melissa, I am not creative at all. I don't know how to draw. My stick people even look silly when I draw them. What if the drawing looks stupid?" Jim anxiously replied.

"I want to remind you that this is something for yourself," I told him. "You don't have to show me what the drawing looks like. You can make the drawing as simple as you'd like. You can do it in pencil or colored markers. This is for you. To help you bring to life your intention in a way that will serve you as you are moving forward on your path. Pretend that you are eight years old again and sitting on the floor coloring and drawing. Bring some fun into it. There is no wrong way to do it and no judgment with it."

After our session together, Jim took a plain piece of white paper and drew a picture of the ocean with a ship in the waters and a sun in the sky. The ocean was a deep blue color that was filled with waves. In the middle of the ocean he drew a picture of the ship, the ship that represented himself. He wanted to remind himself that there would be waves that will try to knock him off track during his journey, but that doesn't have to make him lost or to take on water to sink. The ship looked like an old, wooden pirate ship that could withstand many battles. It had three sets of sails to guide him through the windy journey at sea. In the middle of the drawing at the bottom, he drew a compass with the needle facing north and colored in red. Any time he feels he is getting lost he can take a look at the compass to bring him back to where he's going. He also added luscious green trees on the shore with the sun shining bright in the distance.

Jim was hesitant to create a drawing of his intention when we talked about it during his session, but he took on the task and did it. In a later session, he commented to me about the benefit that he had gotten from taking the time to do the drawing. He was able to look back at the drawing along with his intention statement when he was feeling like he was going off course again. It was a good visual reminder of the path he wanted to take moving forward.

I Am Statements

I want you to know that you are equipped with enough tools for the journey ahead. Even when we feel that we don't know what lies ahead, we have all we need inside of us. I think that sometimes all we need is a reminder of what is already inside of us, and then we can embrace all that we are already, focus on what we already are in the present moment. To do this, I love writing I Am statements. I Am statements are simply written sentences about ourselves that we know are true or have heard from others that they know are true about us. I did this exercise during my journey of becoming a coach. It helped me remember and become grounded in who I am. We don't take enough time in our lives to remind ourselves what we have inside us already. We are quick to say negative things about ourselves and others, but not too many times do you hear someone say anything positive about themselves. Even I admit that I don't walk around telling people that I am creative or I am courageous, but if I mess up at something, then I will say that that was stupid of me to do that.

To give you an example of what I mean by writing I Am statements, I want to share with you the I Am statements that I made those years ago during my journey of gaining clarity. The way that I originally did it was by creating art like my client Jim did with his drawing of his intention. You don't have to do it by creating art or by any other medium if you are not inclined, but I wanted to share with you my whole experience around my I Am statements.

I am *ready*.

I am *strong*.

I am *blessed*.

I am *capable*.

I am *a believer*.

I am *powerful.*

I am *beautiful.*

I am *courageous.*

I am *full of energy.*

I am *full of life.*

I am *whole.*

I am *alive.*

I am *worth it.*

I am *ME.*

Now it is your turn to write I Am statements. You can write as many as you want. My suggestion is to write at least 10 I Am statements. They can be about different character traits that you have, things you admire about yourself, and things that other people compliment you on or say to you. You don't have to 100% believe that they are true, but if a portion of you believes it, then write it down. The portion of you that believes will grow as you continue to read them and say them. It goes back to the saying of faking it 'til you make it. There is scientific truth behind this in our neurobiology. For example, try to fake a smile right now, even if you aren't happy. Our brains are hard-wired in a specific way so that when it's activated, corresponding physiological responses and emotional feelings will follow and you will feel happy.

After you are finished writing your I Am statements, you aren't quite done yet with them. I want you to take the list you have and stand up. You can do this in front of someone else or alone. You may also want to say it in front of a mirror. I want you to stand proudly and state each of these sentences one at a time. Embody each one more and more deeply as you read through the list and as you are filling your heart with praises. Your praises.

You are Ready! You are Capable! You are Courageous! You are Worth It! You may notice some hesitation as you are reading them. That is ok and to be expected. We don't go around every day expressing positive things about ourselves to others or even to ourselves. Don't give up or get discouraged with it. My request is for you to put this list of I Ams on your mirror or your wall at work. Integrate this into your daily routine. You deserve to live fully in your sparkling, authentic light.

When Lisa started working with me, I explained I Am statements and gave her a few examples. I asked her during one of our phone sessions to name 10 I Am statements.

"You want me to name 10 I Am statements about myself?! I thought you were going to ask me to write two or three down. That I can do," Lisa said.

"Ok. Let's start there. Write down two or three that you feel comfortable with," I replied.

I could hear Lisa taking a deep breath on the other side of the phone. She took a couple of minutes to write down her I Am statements. I asked her if she wanted to share them with me. It would help to grow the statements inside of her, bringing them to life.

"Alright, here I go. I was actually able to write down six I Am statements. I'm surprised I was able to come up with more,"

Lisa said. She paused for a moment before she said her I Am statements. I realized the bravery that it took for her to say those statements aloud. She said them to me one at a time, "I am strong. I am loving. I am creative. I am hungry. I am motivated. I am feisty. Were those ok?"

"Those were amazing! Great job!" I said to Lisa. "I'm very proud of you for stepping into the moment and saying your statements to me aloud!"

I asked Lisa to continue to think of more I Am statements that she could add to her already wonderful list. I told her to think of things that loved ones say to her about herself and to add those to the others.

In this chapter, you set the stage for your journey by writing an intention to help plant the seed. You embodied the intention to further ingrain the intention in your mind, body, and soul. You took the time to write I Am statements to see what you were already equipped with. Reading these I Am statements over and over again throughout your journey will even further etch these statements in your neurobiology to become a bigger reality than the space they hold at the present moment.

CHAPTER 5
ON THE HUNT FOR PASSIONS AND VALUES

*"Keep your values positive, because your
values become your destiny."*

MAHATMA GANDHI, *Open Your Mind,
Open Your Life: A Book of Eastern Wisdom*

Do you enjoy getting naked in your everyday life? Now that you sent your intentions out into the universe, it is time to get naked. I want you to strip down and get vulnerable about figuring out what you really want. We will be examining you from the inside out, finding what you are passionate about and evaluating your values.

Pivotal Moments

As we go through life many things happen to us that are pivotal points in our lives. Ones that change who we are inside. We all go through rough times in our lives, and they can either define who we are and change us to become stronger, or they can break us down. Either way, we pick ourselves back up and put the pieces back together – perhaps not in the same way as before, but they still hold us together.

For me, one of the most pivotal moments in my life to get me to where I am today was definitely my brain injury. It stopped me in my tracks and forced me to re-evaluate my whole life and figure out how to put myself back together in a way that would serve me best moving forward. That is what I want you to take a moment to check in on with yourself now. What is a pivotal moment in your life? Maybe for you it is a divorce or getting laid off from your job. If there are multiple pivotal points in your life, note all of them. It doesn't have to be the one that hurt the most or the one that created the most havoc in your life. Also, it doesn't have to be negative. I've mentioned all negative events so far, but it could be when you had a baby or got a promotion at work that required you to move across the United States away from everything that you were familiar with.

When these instances happen in our lives, there is usually a level of fear that comes with it. It could be a good fear or a negative fear. You pushed through it anyway, whether you had a choice or not. That is a big feat. Now here we are back in the present moment. Fear will always be there, it is our reaction and the way we interact with it that can change the way the outcome forms.

There was a question, even before my brain injury happened, that I used to ask myself to help me push the boundaries a little more. How would I *be* if I weren't afraid? I don't believe I would've gotten to the place I am right now after my brain injury without keeping this question in the forefront. If I weren't courageous, brave, and resilient, then I probably wouldn't be sitting here writing this book. I probably wouldn't be as far along in my healing journey if I wasn't a persistent learner and determined to find my path. So how would you *be* if you weren't afraid? The answer to this question will be key for you in going through this. Keep these being words in your forefront of your mind.

What Drives You?

What do you notice drives you in life? What is something that gets your juices flowing, something that makes you want to wake up in the morning and rush to do it? It doesn't have to be what you are doing for work, and odds are it probably isn't if you currently are feeling unfulfilled in the work you are doing. This might be a hard question to answer. Think of hobbies that you enjoy doing, or it could be just the act of helping others. I know when I am doing something that will help others I am more driven in the task even if the task isn't very stimulating. It also doesn't have to be a tangible thing that you are doing. When I have a deadline for something, whether it is self-imposed or set by someone else, I notice that it drives me and gets me motivated to do it. If I am doing something where there is no deadline, a part of me gets lackadaisical and the effort that I put forth withers away. These subtle items will be good to note now and will be of use to you later in the chapter.

Inner Journey Exercises

When I was in coaching training at CTI, there were two exercises on our inner journey towards finding our life purpose whose results still stick out in my mind. I want to do these exercises with you, then I will share with you what showed itself in my experience. To me, this helped to see where my mindset was and where it wanted me to go.

The first journey you will be going on is to imagine yourself on a stage in front of a large group of people. There is a buzz in the space. You look out over the crowd. Feel the feelings you're having as you are about to address the gathering. Just as you step up to the microphone, time freezes for an instant and you hear a voice in your ear that says your name and then says, "In the next 30 seconds you will have a chance to have any impact you want on this entire group. It will be only one chance, one impact, but all of these people will be changed in some way; they will have a different life because of the impact you had on them. Thirty seconds. Ready, go. 30, 29, 28, 27 ... 10, 9, 8, 7, 6, 5, 4, 3, 2, 1."

Now I want you to take a moment to close your eyes and visualize this happening, going up onto a stage in front of a large crowd and looking out over them. Then imagine having that whisper in your ear. What would you say to this group of people for the next 30 seconds to have an impact on them and change their lives forever?

After you take the time to visualize yourself giving this speech to the group of people, I want you to note: What impact did you have on the crowd? How were you and everyone else transformed by the speech? Who were you being in that space to have such an impact? You may be shocked at the impact that you had on the crowd. Did you have any idea what words were going to come out of you during that speech?

When I did this exercise, I was really astounded by the size of the crowd and where I was when I gave my speech. The speech itself was also not what I was expecting at the time. Looking back on it now, it all makes perfect sense, which is why I want to share it with you. What we think and speak can come true when we put the energy towards it. During my inner journey, I was on a stage at the National Mall in Washington D.C. with a group of 200,000 people. For those of you who don't know the National Mall, it is the area between the Lincoln Memorial and the United States Capitol Building. I was standing on a 300-foot metal stage at the base of the Washington Monument facing the Capitol Building with the crowd gathered on the grassy green lawn between the two structures. I spoke to the crowd about how many of us are waiting to get hit over the head by the universe with a wake-up call at some point in our lives. We need to stop being ok with "average," and we need to live what we are meant to be. The audience was awestruck by all that I said to them. I am working my way to making this happen one day.

The second exercise I want you to visualize is that you've been given a billboard, and you can put any message on it. Thousands of people will drive by and see your billboard each day. What does it say? I want you to go with the first thought that comes to you from your gut. This is an exercise that can be overthought, and your head can begin to get in the way. Take a moment, close your eyes, take a few deep breaths, and visualize yourself driving past your billboard. What does the billboard reveal to you?

After you do the exercise, take note: What did you observe about your billboard? Was it colorful? Did it have a fancy design on it? How big was it? Did it contain only words or a phrase?

When I did the exercise, my billboard read: *You were not born to live a mediocre life.* That message was meant for me as much as it was meant for the thousands of people that were going to be driving past that billboard each day. I was starting to see a theme in those inner journey exercises. I was meant for something bigger in my life than what I was currently living. Being an everyday average Joe was not the path I was supposed to be on. Not that there is anything wrong with being average, but I was seeing that I wasn't supposed to play in that arena anymore. My seed was planted to bloom in a bigger garden. What theme are you noticing that is starting to arise from the two inner journey exercises that we did? Does it tie back into your intention that you set in Chapter 4?

Repairing Your Inner Compass

We are beginning to build the momentum to find out what your passions are in life and where you might want to go to start filling that hole and get out of stuck status. What are you willing to try to get to this new place? With trying comes risk. It also involves stepping into or leaning into the process and having trust. And, as with everything, when you start something new there is always a process of letting go of something else. What is it time to heal?

We lost our way along the path and we need to use our inner compass to find our way back to heading in the right direction, just like the one Jim used in his drawing. Your compass might need a small repair after what you have gone through. Let's take the time now to repair it and find what you are missing.

One of the ways I like to begin to repair the compass is by looking at our values. Life gets in the way, and we can forget the values that we hold. To me, our values are the recipe for our lives. They are who you are and how you want to show up in life. When you live a life in alignment with your values, it is fulfilling. How about we begin to mine for your values. What are some obvious values that you hold? They might include respect, honesty, loyalty, trust. What else do you value? When you are standing in the place of clear knowing, what values do you know to be true? Authenticity, freedom, vulnerability? Another way to find your values is by asking yourself what makes you angry. What value is getting stepped on when you get angry? Who do you admire and what values do they hold that you admire in them?

Living in our values is a step that we can take to repair our compass. How do you feel after identifying the values that you hold? If you had to pick your top three values, what would they be? It is hard to narrow down our values to the top three, but see what you come up with. Are these values being stepped on in your life currently? Meaning, are any of your top three values absent from your life? This is a huge discovery if you notice any one of these values being absent in any area of your life. It contributes to that hole inside of you, that stuckness, and the damaging of your inner compass.

My top three values are trust, freedom, and authenticity. But when I was working at the CPA firm as an auditor, my values of freedom and authenticity were absent. I was extremely unfulfilled, and that caused that hole inside me. Two of my top three values were being stepped on like they didn't matter. I felt stuck not enjoying the work, but not knowing what I wanted to do otherwise. I wasn't able to do what I wanted when I wanted to, so my freedom value was squashed. As I mentioned in Chapter 2, I felt like a fraud because I hated the work I was doing, so I wasn't living in authenticity.

There might be aspects of your life where you are standing firmly in all three of your top values. It could be in your relationships; it could be at work. When I stand in my top values, I feel like I am on cloud nine. When I think about all three of these values being honored all at once in my life, I feel unstoppable, like I am capable of doing anything I put my mind to and can excel in all areas of my life. Even when I stand in each value separately, they all hold their ground. Having my own life coaching business, helping other people realize their worth, and helping them go from stuck to gaining clarity and playing bigger in their lives checks off each of my top three values.

Values Exploration

What part of you do you want to honor in moving forward? It might be one or all three of the values that you just identified. If any of your values are not currently being honored that would be one to focus on. You will be using this value in the visualization that you will be doing next.

Join me in this next exploration. Take the value that you just picked that you want to honor in moving forward. Got it in your head? Perfect. You don't need anything else with you in this exercise. Whatever room you are in is the room you are meant to be in for this exploration. First, take a moment to look around the room at all of the furniture, pictures, objects, and anything else that might be there. I want you to find something in the room that represents the value that you picked to honor. For example, you might have picked the value respect. What in the room represents the value respect to you? Do that with your value you chose. What is it about this item that symbolizes the value for you? I want you to focus in on this item alone. Embody what this item symbolizes for you in your body. What are you feeling? What is coming alive for you? Let yourself experience this value through this object. What do you notice is possible living this value? In contrast, who are you not being by not connecting with this value?

I want to share with you a time I did this exploration with a client of mine, Beth. The value that Beth wanted to honor was freedom. She was sitting in her dining room during our coaching call. There was a dining room table, a chandelier light fixture hanging above the table, and a wooden floor. The room had a carpet that was big enough to cover the length of the table and chairs. The item that she picked to represent freedom was the carpet. It had multiple shades of blue, green, red, and purple in it. It was sprinkled with designs. The carpet immediately stuck out to her as the object to pick. Having her just mention the carpet I could already hear excitement in her voice. Her energy shot up a few notches. I asked her to describe the carpet and where she got it. Her mother had gotten it for her when she went on one of her trips. When I asked her to embody the feeling of freedom in the carpet and describe the feeling for me, she lit up even more. She described the shapes and colors and how there was not an exact pattern in it. It followed its own way. There were squiggles that would weave back and forth along the carpet and just stop at any time. The shapes were different colors and sizes. Not one was like any other. As she was describing it, I could picture the carpet myself as if it were right in front of me.

When I asked her what was possible in living in this value of freedom, she mentioned that she would be able to let go of the step-by-step approach that she was used to following. That she would be able to get back to the painting she used to do over 10 years ago. Her circumstances in life had stopped her from doing what she loved, and it had just compounded over the years. Now, it didn't matter what was going on, she wanted to start painting again. It was an outlet for her, and she wanted it back. By not connecting to this value of freedom, it felt as if part of her was missing. She got caught up in her everyday life and lost part of herself. She went out after we got off the call to go get supplies to start painting again.

Did you have a similar experience to Beth's?

Before my brain injury occurred, I couldn't imagine what I was passionate about. I knew that I enjoyed doing many things, but never recognized any of them as a passion. It was as if something died inside of me, and I couldn't hear or recognize the inner voice inside me screaming at me to slow down and identify what I was missing in my life, that I wasn't honoring my top values. But there was a time when I must have heard my inner voice, even though I didn't recognize it as such, when I quit my job to go backpacking around Europe. That was a time when I felt most fulfilled. I was living in my truth and feeling the freedom and authenticity all at the same time. Can you think back to a time when you felt fulfilled? Did you listen to that inner voice whispering in your ear?

Passions Inventory

It is time to get into your heart and take inventory of what you are passionate about. This is supposed to be a brain dump of anything and everything that comes to mind that ignites something inside of you. I find it easiest to give clients a list of questions to help spark things that they are passionate about and start building their inventory. As you read the following questions, know that there is no right or wrong way of doing it. You can use these questions as a guide, or come up with your own to answer.

What have I always been good at?

What did I want to be growing up?

What idea did my parents or teachers squash in my younger years?

What makes me most fulfilled?

What do I love to do most?

What calling is showing up in my heart right now?

What do I want to be remembered for?

What do I know how to do?

How can I help people get what they want?

Is there a frustration in the world that I feel I can help solve?

Who do I admire most?

What needs do I care about most?

Pinpointing the pivotal moments in your life will help show you where shifts happened and pieces of you changed inside and out. These moments could be part of what drives you in your life. You went on two inner journeys, each revealing messages about what you want to show yourself and the world. You took the time to repair your inner compass and explore what is important in your life. Then you did a passions inventory brain dump using the questions provided to list the things that you are passionate about. This inventory will provide a basis for you as you begin to narrow down those passions and gain clarity on the direction to take going forward.

CHAPTER 6
ATTAINING CLARITY

*"Your vision will become clear only when you
can look into your own heart... Who looks
outside, dreams; who looks inside, awakes."*

CARL JUNG

We get many whispers along our journey trying to get us to change paths, but we are too afraid to listen to them. That is why I love this quote from Brené Brown: "The universe is not short on wake-up calls. We're just quick to hit the snooze button." There were countless times where I had wake-up calls coming at me, but I kept hitting the snooze button until that day in 2012 when I was hit in the head with a softball for the fourth time. Hopefully that will be the last time. I kept hitting snooze. For what reason? You probably have similar scenarios in your life. Odds are you weren't hit in the head with a softball multiple times, but what do you notice keeps happening to you to get you to finally stop and wake up?

Passions Presented to You

At the end of the last chapter, you were going to take the time to write down what you were passionate about and brainstorm all that came to your mind using those questions I supplied. What came up for you? Were there any surprises? Years ago, when I did the exercise, I had some surprises and other thoughts that I realized had always been in the back of my mind, but I hadn't paid much attention to them. Some examples: I was passionate about working in fraud, catching people for bad things they do. I enjoyed listening to others and comforting them. I liked helping others through tough situations. I also wrote down that I would like to be there for juveniles who are hurting from situations growing up and help them start to believe in themselves.

Taking the list of things you are passionate about, what would you say is your relationship to them? Do they make you excited or feel love inside? There might be a feeling of risk involved or a fear around them, maybe even a resistance around some of them because you don't know how you would even be able to get started in doing it. What are you noticing?

Some of the items may have a greater pull on you than others. The others might be more of a hobby to you. What piece are you seeing is your area of quiet desperation, a place where, if you don't start to make a movement, it will continue to grow that hole inside of you? There is something tugging at your heartstrings. It may be associated with an incident that happened in your past or a love for something that you have always wanted to do, but never had the guts to go after. In all of us, if we begin to listen to that wake-up call, that area of quiet desperation inside begins to break up, preparing itself as fertile ground for growth.

What Would You Do If You Weren't Afraid?

Before my injury, a friend and I often used this saying to help us begin to play bigger: What would you *do* if you weren't afraid? I can't remember the origin of where I heard this, but we were both unhappy with our jobs and in our lives and we would use this to help us take more chances. I used to write it on my hand every day to push my thinking and myself. So I'm asking you, what would you do if you weren't afraid? If you trusted that thing that is pulling at your heartstrings to do, what would you be doing? Just explore this and be bold about it. There is no commitment to having to do it. It could be starting a new charity foundation for a cause that you love, or working to get the laws changed to deliver harsher punishments for people that commit child abuse. Maybe you have always wanted to go back to school to get your doctorate, or go for that license in the field you are in, but have been too afraid of failure.

I posed this question to Maria when I worked with her. I asked her to think about what she was passionate about in life and to push the fear aside when pondering the question, "What would you do if you weren't afraid?"

"Well, I would probably get another job," Maria answered. "I don't care for what I am doing right now. It would be nice to get a job where I could work from home so I can be around my dog and be able to walk him during the day. I get home too late at night during the week, so my husband usually has to be the one to do it."

I could feel the fear come over her when I asked her that question. She wanted another job, but she was too afraid to even say what type of job that she wanted. This is a natural reaction. I reminded her that with this exercise, she didn't have to make any commitments to what she was saying she would do if she wasn't afraid. So I posed the question to her again, asking her to really think about what she would do if fear wasn't stopping her and she wasn't afraid to fail.

"If I knew I was able to do it, I would love to write a series of fiction books. I would travel the world doing book signings and talking to people about them," Maria replied. "But I would have to think about my husband and what he was doing and whether it would work with his schedule."

"Maria, I noticed that after you stated you would write a series of fiction books, your fear crept in again, and you snuck back into your comfort zone using your husband as a reason why you might not be able to do it," I said. "Remember, no commitment to needing to go do this work. What other things would get you excited to do if you weren't afraid?"

"I would love to open a dog shelter. I love dogs! I got my dog from a shelter and to be able to help other dogs, I would be so happy."

I don't think Maria realized how excited she was when she talked about opening a dog shelter. The sound of her voice and the look on her face were priceless. Something was ignited inside of her. I asked her if she noticed the excitement she exuded as she spoke those words about the dog shelter. She said that she always wanted to work in a dog shelter, she just always put it on the back burner. It was at this point when Maria began to start building a relationship with her passions to see where this took her on her path.

When I did this exercise, there were similarities to the list I wrote of what I was passionate about, but I saw that other things emerged to push me out of my comfort zone to do them. The one that was similar was to work one-on-one or in a group with juveniles to open the path of communication. I want to use my gift of being able to see the person behind the mask. I could open a business. Become a life coach or a trainer. I could go back to school to become a forensic psychologist or criminal investigator, or get my doctorate in psychology. And – this was an outlier – I've always wanted to have a role in television or a movie.

Build a Relationship with Your Passions

You want to start building a relationship with these passions that are beginning to grow in front of you. You want to start to hang out with them and get to know them, as they are a part of you. How can you nourish these parts of you that lay dormant for a long time? What do you do when you first meet someone else? You ask how they are doing and ask questions to get to know them. What would it look like to do that with your passions? Find common ground to begin to feed this relationship. This takes us back to when you set your intention in the beginning of your journey. You planted the seed, having it take root. The seed is now beginning to sprout. As with any plant, it needs care and attention to continue to grow and blossom. You need to ensure the correct amount of sunlight hits it, and make sure it has enough water to grow, but not so much that it floods the plant and the roots die. What else could you do to take care of this plant that is beginning to sprout? Tying this back in with your passions, what does this uncover for you about how you can be in relationship with them? And the benefit to doing this?

Reframing Old Beliefs

Now that you have this seed beginning to sprout into a plant, you probably are wondering how you continue to feed this plant so it doesn't die. Ok, so you have these ideas of what to do next, now what? You don't have everything you need right now to fulfill your passion, so you feel stuck. In the past, when you had thoughts of doing something else, what beliefs did you hold about what you needed to get started that were detrimental or unhelpful in pursuing your passion further? For example, you might be thinking that you need to go get your doctorate, or that you need to be more outgoing and confident.

I know that in the past, I thought I had to have big connections with people in high places to get where I needed to go. I thought it would take too much time to get there, so trying was pointless. Like the rest of society, which wants things right now for immediate satisfaction, I wanted to go from zero to 100 in an instant.

There is a powerful tool we use in the coaching world called reframing: taking something bad that happens and looking at it as a positive thing. For example, my brain injury happened and I wasn't able to go back to work, but I was able to take the time to find something to do with my life that is fulfilling. What does it look like if you come up with a reframe for the detrimental beliefs that you once held or continue to hold? Three of the new reframing ideas that I used were that I could take baby steps, that Rome wasn't built in a day, and that I could start learning to coach alongside my paid work and that it didn't have to be all or nothing. These helped me believe that the things I wanted were actually possible to attain, that I wouldn't have to uproot my entire life to get the life that I felt I deserved. It helped having a life coach to support me and to give me little nudges when I would fall trying to take those baby steps. It helped me in knowing that my journey was achievable. I knew it would take time to do what I wanted to do, and that I wasn't yet the person I needed to be to do this passion. I needed to grow my mindset and also grow my skill set. You will get there, just as I did. You have to remember that it is a process. The mailroom clerk doesn't become the CEO of the company overnight.

Giving Yourself Permission

You are probably having some limiting beliefs that are keeping you from moving forward. To grow my mindset, one of the things I still do today is give myself permission. We follow so many strict rules in life about how we are supposed to be or what we are supposed to do that we put our minds into a box. We begin to believe that we have to be a certain way. In the process that follows, we are going to break those rules.

I want you to give yourself permission to do what you want, be who you need to be so you can get to that next level of becoming the person you are meant to be and bringing your passion out into the world. The world needs what you want to offer and give them. It is waiting for you to grow into that person so you can share it. To do this, I want you to create a permission slip just like in elementary school when your parents had to sign something allowing you to go to the zoo for the day. It has the same premise. To continue moving forward toward filling that hole inside of you and gaining the life you've always wanted, what do you want to give yourself permission to be or do? Perhaps you are working in a very business-like environment and it's not proper to show your feelings and be vulnerable, so you want to give yourself permission to be vulnerable. You can create a permission slip for as many things as you feel you need to give yourself permission for. What do you need to start doing or stop doing? I want you to take the time to write down these permissions that you are giving to yourself. They are massive gifts to yourself. Get as creative as you want when making them. You could write them down in a journal or do it old school on small slips of paper. Write them out stating that you have permission to be ... whatever you want it to say. We are giving ourselves permission in order to remind us that it's okay to do things differently until we begin to build up those new neural pathways in our brains of our new ways of being and it becomes a pattern. Therefore, I ask that you place these permission slips in a place where you will be able to see them every day. You can put them at your desk at work or hang them on your refrigerator. See what works for you.

My client, Barbara, found these permission slips really powerful. She had never felt like she had permission, and the mindset shift that it created in her was life-changing. A nurse working long hours, she realized she was unhappy in her career. She was making good money and helping others, but she didn't feel satisfied. It was causing her unhappiness and she realized that over the years she had let herself go. She had started gaining a lot of weight, and her dissatisfaction with that added to the hole that she was feeling at work. She desperately needed to give herself permission to be and do certain things to begin to change the patterns that had been drawn in her life.

I had her write permission slips, which she loved. Besides writing them on slips of paper, she wrote them on her mirror with dry erase markers. That way, each time she went in the bathroom and looked in the mirror, she was reminded of what she was giving herself permission to be and do. She gave herself permission to be vulnerable and self-compassionate. She found nursing emotionally draining. She had to hold it together while working with sick patients, and she noticed that she wasn't allowing herself to be vulnerable outside of work to talk about what had upset her during the day. She showed everyone else compassion, but never took the time to show herself the same compassion she gave to others. That was big one for her. She realized that she also needed to give herself permission to be healthy. Just because she saw sick people everyday didn't mean that she had to feel bad that she wasn't sick. She was allowed to be healthy. She gave herself permission to work out to help her feel stronger and better about herself. What a gift she gave herself by doing these permissions!

To get a better idea of what you might want to have in your permission slips, here is a sample of permission slips that my clients have written.

- I give myself permission to be courageous.

- I give myself permission to be confident and believe in myself.

- I give myself permission to free up my time for things that bring me joy.

- I give myself permission to fail.

- I give myself permission to look for other jobs.

- I give myself permission to spend money on things that help me further pursue my passion.

- I give myself permission to be afraid of taking the next step.

Giving yourself permission allows you to go from where you are to where you want to be. What do you want to allow more of into your life? Who do you need to be in order to get there? It is the process of crossing that bridge to work your way towards getting to the other side. You are starting to sew up that hole that is deep within you. By giving yourself permission, you are freeing up a part of you that was not available up to this point. It opens up the possibilities of what direction for you to go.

Clearing the Fog Visualization

I want to take you on a journey, guide you through a visualization, to this clearing and to gain clarity. If you have a trustworthy person in your life to read you this visualization, it will allow you to close your eyes and actually do the visualization. If not, that is ok. If you get stuck or distracted during the visualization, try to do it at another time when you are more relaxed and are able to slow down.

You can begin by closing your eyes or having a soft gaze looking off in the distance. Take a few deep breaths and relax into whatever position you are currently in, sitting up or lying down – whatever is comfortable to you. With each exhale, release any tension you have in your body, starting with your feet. Next, move up to your legs. Breathing in and out, softening your muscles. In the exhale, release any stress in your stomach, then back. Watch the stress as it floats away out of your body. And as you continue to breathe in, breathe in calmness and ease. Release any tension in your neck perhaps by rolling your neck and bringing your attention now to your arms and fingers. Relax more into your space, softening your jaw and tongue. Now, if you would, bring your attention to your mind's eye. Using your mind's eye, bring to mind a picture of you walking in the woods. As you begin to walk, you see a path that is encircled by a tunnel of trees. You continue walking on the path into the tunnel of trees. You notice that the path is wide enough for a car to drive on it. The tunnel of trees is creating this darkness in front of you. It's as though you are walking through a foggy morning. If you notice that the path is too dark, then allow yourself to carry a lantern that will give you light along the way. You are walking down the middle of this stone-laid path. The stones are smooth, creating a massaging action against your feet as you walk along.

You may notice the silence that is accompanying you on your journey, allowing you to be in deep reflection and thought as you are walking on the path. You are safe in your surroundings and free to be able to walk this path. As you begin to walk this path, what are you noticing along the way? Do you see any animals in the trees or on the path? Are there any carvings in the trees or feelings that come up as you are walking? Can you feel the temperature of the air as you are breathing it in? Or are there any smells that are familiar to you?

And as you continue to walk along the path, you are reminded of the journey that you have been on so far in life. You might be recalling memories from childhood or your last job. Let the memories pass through you without letting them take hold of you. Just notice what is coming up for you. Notice the smooth stones you are walking on as you begin to note the intention that you set for yourself in the beginning of this new journey. Do you see it written in words? Maybe it is represented by a symbol of some sort.

The heavy fog is still set in on the path. Looking around now as you continue moving down the path through the tunnel of trees, you see the values that you identified that are important to you. Maybe they are the top three values that you identified, or perhaps you notice other words highlighting themselves in the woods. Are the words passing in front of you or along the sides of the path? As you look from side to side, there might be other ones further within the woods that you notice. What might those be identified as?

You are wearing a backpack, and inside are the permission slips that you wrote to free yourself in this journey. Stop for a minute as you are continuing to breathe to take those permission slips out. Read each of the permission slips slowly, one at a time to remind yourself what you need to give yourself permission to be and do along the way. As you look up from the permission slips, you notice that the fog is starting to give way. You are nearing the end of the tunnel of trees.

In the clearing ahead there is a stump of a tree. I want you to walk up to the stump and see what is waiting for you there. On the stump of that tree is a picture or a symbol or a word that helps you see the next steps of your journey. You may not understand it right now when seeing it, but it is your guide to help you move forward in your journey. It could represent one of your passions that you identified or a dream that you have. Whatever is waiting for you on the stump, accept it as a token for you in taking this journey to fill that hole you have inside. There is an appreciation in it giving you wisdom and guidance. This is your parting gift from the universe.

After receiving your gift, you can make your way into the vast fields of green ahead of you. There is an open space for you to grow and use this gift that you just received. Take a moment to enjoy what you have been given. Run in the fields with the butterflies. Maybe kick a ball around. Then pause for a minute to lie down in the grass. Slowing time down to receive what you have been given, look up and take in the sun's heat and the blue sky above.

As you are breathing in, give thanks to the universe and to yourself for having the courage to be on this journey. Then take a second to add anything else you want to say in appreciation. Know that your life will be different from this point forward. You can begin to bring your attention and awareness back into the room by wiggling your toes and moving your hands. Slowly come back into your body, feeling the chair or the floor beneath you. When you are ready, open your eyes and journal about your experience that you had. Use the questions below to guide you in your journaling:

> What did you notice about your intention? How was it represented?

> What values revealed themselves to you? How were they shown to you?

> What gift did you receive on the stump?

> What surprised you about this experience?

> What different perspective do you have now from what you were previously operating with?

In this chapter you reviewed the passions from the brain dump and noted any surprises from the list you created. Then you pondered the question, "What would you do if you weren't afraid?" and noted the answers. This hopefully further narrowed down your passions toward gaining more clarity on your next steps. By building a relationship with your passions, you get to understand them more. Your plant is beginning to sprout. It is very helpful to use the coaching tool of reframing to shift your mindset on the limiting beliefs that have been holding you back from moving forward in doing your passions. Then, by giving yourself permission in areas of your life where you haven't been allowing space or room to breathe, you got a jolt of energy to continue forward on a more meaningful track. Lastly, you did the clearing the fog visualization, taking you on a journey to uncover your path ahead. You received a gift from the universe on the tree stump at the end of the tunnel. Hold this precious gift close to you as you continue to gain clarity on your next steps.

CHAPTER 7

READY FOR THE LEAP

"Do one thing every day that scares you."

ELEANOR ROOSEVELT

olleen started working with me and dove into the S.O.A.R.I.N.G. process, being open to what presented itself to her. A financial analyst who dreamed of working in the mental health field, she was excited about an upcoming presentation – until she practiced it in front of three of her friends. Afterward, when she was lying in bed and replaying the evening over and over in her head, she thought, "I really sucked tonight. I sounded like I didn't know anything on the subject even though I live it. I talked in circles. I basically read from the PowerPoint slides. I will never be able to find the job I want." She tossed and turned in bed that evening, when an image of the clearing the fog visualization that we did together popped into her head, making her feel like she was still in the fog, especially after that night.

Colleen called me the next morning and said, "Melissa, I was horrific last night practicing the presentation with my friends. I just don't think I can go after my dream. I should probably quit now and continue with my work as an analyst."

I reminded Colleen that this is part of the process. I asked her to think about the gift that she received from the universe from her clearing the fog visualization and the new path she wants to take moving forward. I asked her to tell me three good things that she got from doing her presentation.

"I haven't taken the time to think about the good things," she said. But then, after a moment, she continued, "Alright, I realized last night that I do love speaking in front of people, even though it felt like I just read from the slides. My friends did say they learned a lot about anxiety and the health risks of having it from listening to my story and the health facts I presented. It made me curious about what I could do with this, like as a career. I guess that is my third thing."

As Colleen did in her work with me, you will be focusing on the path that you want to take now moving forward. You will be taking the first step on this new path by writing down your targets and going after them. I also see a leap in your future. I will be introducing to you the concept of leaping, in which you will be doing a leap and gaining feedback for yourself.

A New Awareness

The path to take might not be as crystal clear as you want it to be. There may still be a few options for you that you might want to take. It is still messy and that is okay. At this point, we don't need you to know the exact destination, just having a better idea of what general direction the new path will take. You begin to have a new awareness in your conscious of what is tugging at you on the inside to do, whether it was something that you knew when you were younger that you wanted to do and lost sight of or it was something that birthed itself through one of your pivotal moments in your life. With this new awareness comes responsibility. You are aware of the need for more of this in the world.

Whether one clear passion emerges for you or you are weighing more than one, you are seeing the need. You are feeling it and you are beginning to know that you have a responsibility to do something about it. You may feel that you can no longer sit around and let your life go on without taking action. If you haven't been able to narrow your passion down to one thing after your visualization and the work you have done so far in the journey, don't worry – we'll work on it.

When I was heading out in my new direction after my brain injury, I narrowed my journey down to two potential paths. I didn't know which one was best for me. I knew that I either wanted to become a therapist, like I had wanted to back in college originally, or become a life coach. I knew that I wanted to help people, but I wasn't sure whether I wanted to work with people on problems that stemmed from their past. For that, I would probably have to go back to school to get my master's degree and possibly go on to get my doctorate. Or I could work with people where they were in their current lives and help them see the potential they had in themselves to be their best person moving forward. If I went the life coaching route, then I would have to do research on what I needed to do and probably take classes to get certified.

Possible Targets

With your new awareness from the work you have done up to this point, we can work on targets that you might want to attain. These won't be long-term goals since you are not yet at the point of knowing the exact direction of your journey. If you were to take action today of the options that you are throwing around in your head as possible passions to move forward in doing, what would those be? That is what we are doing with this exercise of writing down targets that you might want to attain. It is a further narrowing down of where you want to be and what you want to be doing. Take the time to note what would make you fulfilled in moving forward, and set that as a target. The target might be scary to you. Notice what feelings are coming up for you as you write down the targets.

The Concept of Leaping

There is a concept that I fell in love with while doing the Playing Big program with Tara Mohr called Leaping. This is a concept of taking action, and it is what propelled me into seeing that I was meant to become a life coach. The definition of a leap, as Tara describes it, is getting into action before your idea is perfect and fully researched. Getting it out there while it's still muddled and undefined. You can use the targets you identified and see which one you are eyeing to go after. I like to think of a leap as planting little seedlings and seeing which one will grow and take root.

When we take on something new, we often find ways to hide from doing it and having to put ourselves out there in the world to be seen. One way we hide is by thinking the plan moving forward has to be perfect before we can do it. If it is not going to work out exactly as we planned then we don't do it. Why do we do that? Because there is fear in the unknown, so if we aren't 100% sure it will work out a certain way then we don't go for it.

We also can hide behind the perceived need for more education, thinking that we have to go get our master's degree so we can learn more about this topic and only then will we be ready. So many people get stuck in the research and education phase that their passion ends up stalled by the need for perfection and for all things to be in alignment.

I want you to not stall in place anymore. It is time to be seen and to try things out. To see if you would enjoy doing your passion before taking the time to make an investment in it. That is what leaping is all about.

The Playing Big program's criteria for doing a leap were useful and powerful measures, so we'll use them here. In doing your leap, make sure that:

1. It is intimately related to your passion.

2. It can be done immediately and finished within two weeks.

3. It will involve obtaining feedback from the people

that you want to influence, meaning your target audience, if your leap pertains to people.

4. It needs to get your adrenaline flowing and get you out of your comfort zone.

If it doesn't make you sweat when thinking of going out and doing it, then it is not a leap. Since it needs to be completed in two weeks, making new products from scratch if you are considering selling something or having an extravagant event if you are thinking of becoming an event promoter will not be good ideas. Simplicity is the key. This leap will help give you the motivation to move forward doing the passion that you identified, taking baby steps forward.

I want you to know that doing a leap can be, and most likely will be, scary. It requires that you step out of your comfort zone. But I am here by your side to make sure that you will succeed at doing your leap. As you think about what to do for your leap, consider this quote from Benjamin Mee in *We Bought a Zoo:* "You know, sometimes all you need is 20 seconds of insane courage. Just literally 20 seconds of just embarrassing bravery. And I promise you, something great will come of it."

If you were able to do something that required only 20 seconds of insane courage, what would you do? Use this to helping with taking your leap.

In doing something scary, fear can set in for you and get in the way of setting your leap. Begin to bounce ideas around in your head. It will help to put them on paper. Think about what type of leap would help get you started in determining if this is the passion that you are meant to do as you move forward on your path.

It is great to have someone who is on your side when thinking about what you want to do for your leap and in taking it. Insane courage is easier to have when you feel supported. Sometimes it also helps to get an outside push from someone else that challenges you to push yourself. Challenges yourself to aim higher in your targets. Gets you outside of your comfort zone of possibilities you are able to attain. Now imagine me as your supporter. I'm there for you, in your corner, as you are getting ready to determine what you are going to do for your leap. What do you wish I'd dare you to do?

Examples of Leaps

Here are some examples of the way that we would usually go about doing something, followed by what I mean by doing a leap. The first way might be what you put as your target in the exercise you did earlier. Notice the difference when we twist it to become a leap that can be completed in the next couple weeks to try it out and gain feedback from your target audience.

- Your target might be to spend the next three months creating classes to teach online to your audience. Turning this into a leap would be to send a message out to your audience today with a free call in a few days about beta classes that you will be teaching starting next week. Then create the classes each week as you go along.

- Going back to school to get your master's or doctorate degree. Turning this into a leap would be going and speaking on what you already know on the subject, or finding a mentor that you would be able to shadow for a day or two to see what a day would be like if that field required the advanced degree.

- Hiring a web designer to make you a website. Turning this into a leap would be going to one of the free website makers out there and using a prebuilt layout to get your About and Contact Us pages completed.

- You might be looking to leave your job in consulting and become a chef cooking Italian food. Turning this into a leap would be to host a cooking class at your house inviting friends, or people that you didn't know who wouldn't be biased, who would be in your target market over to take it and give you feedback. This could help determine whether you want to continue on to culinary school.

My Leap

I want to share with you my leap that I did when I was determining whether I wanted to become a therapist or a coach. This was my plan that I came up with before executing my leap. I was looking to help others improve themselves and help them find their passions in life. That tied to the first criteria of it being intimately related to my passion. I was planning to post an ad to get clients that I could help for free. I wasn't going to make a business plan or an outline. I would meet with them or talk to them a couple times a week for a few weeks. I was going to get feedback from them on how the interaction went to see if it helped them in any way. I was also going to see if it ignited a flame within me and had me wanting more. It would narrow down whether I wanted to go the therapist or the coaching route – or neither.

I closed my eyes and leaped! Here is what happened. I put an ad on Craigslist to see if I could get clients. The ad was addressed to people who wanted to change, and offered free coaching sessions. I wrote that I wasn't a trained therapist or a coach, but I was very intuitive and wanted to work with others on their journey to self-discovery to help them take the next step to find themselves. I let them know in the ad that it would only be for about two to three weeks and that I was requesting feedback to help me start my new endeavor. I didn't know what to expect or if I would get any responses from people. It was scary! That is part of the leap: the vulnerability of putting something out there.

I was extremely shocked that I heard from six people. I thought when I advertised that I was only going to hear from women. Wrong! The majority of the people I heard from were men. The ages ranged from 19 to 60. This was exciting. I realized pretty quickly that I was not meant to be a therapist. My fire inside was being ignited by being with the people where they were currently and helping them to find new discoveries inside them, not by talking through their past and working through it. I was shocked. This wasn't what I was expecting at all. I thought for sure I was going to be validated in my wanting to become a therapist like I wanted to become back in college. Nope, life coach it was.

The feedback I heard from each of them was great in that they were already experiencing shifts inside of them after only two weeks of working with me. I thought, imagine who I could help if I worked with them longer than that! I knew this was my path, but if I never had taken the leap to do this, odds are I would've gone a different route. Since I had in my earlier years in college thought about going into psychology, I probably would've gone the route of a therapist and gone back to school. My leap saved me a lot of money and time. I would probably be in a better place than when I worked as an auditor, but not feeling fully fulfilled as I am today. Thank you, Leap.

You might remember Sally, from Chapter 1, who felt like an undercover fraud at her job completing accounting reports on time while always talking about her love for animals.

I introduced her to the concept of leaping, and she said, "I need to think of a leap that I will be able to do while still being able to work my full-time job, Melissa. I love working with animals and would love to become a vet one day, but I don't know what I would be able to do for my leap that I can complete in a couple weeks."

I said to her, "It sounds like you know that it will pertain to animals. What would get your adrenaline flowing if you were to go out there and do it?"

Sally thought about it for a minute. I wanted her to know that I would be there by her side so she could push herself in the leap that she was thinking about doing.

"Ok. So there are a few that come to mind," she said. "I could go to an animal shelter and see if I could help out there. Also, my veterinarian knows me pretty well since I have so many pets, and I'm taking each of them in regularly to get their shots and to make sure that they are healthy. He would probably let me come in one day over the weekend to see what he does during his appointments with the animals. And the other one, I haven't told many people this, but I've always wanted to have my own dog-boarding place."

"Sally, is your heart racing at the thought of owning a dog-boarding place? I can feel it from here. What would be a leap that you would be able to do around boarding dogs?" I said back to her.

"Holy cow! Are you joking?! This is crazy! I need to take a deep breath. I don't know if I can do this," Sally exclaimed. "Wow. Ok. I could ask the lady who boards my dogs when I go out of town if I can help her out the next couple weekends. She doesn't live too far away from me so it shouldn't be that bad."

"Perfect! How does that feel to say the words of your leap? To be able to jump into it to see if this is something that you would want to do?" I asked. "I want to acknowledge that it is scary and you are brave and courageous for going after what you want. You will never know unless you take the chance."

"I know. I'm afraid, but I am excited," Sally replied. "I will get to spend the weekend around dogs! I will also get to learn more about what goes into having a dog-boarding business."

Learning from Your Leap

We use the concept and action of doing a leap to learn. It helps us to learn more about what we want to do. It might help you determine which path you want to take like it did for Sally and me. It helped me realize that I wanted to go into one field over another. It helped Sally see that she had the right field of working with animals, but instead of healing animals, she is boarding animals. It can also help you learn more about your target audience, if your passion requires one.

For example, you might think in doing your leap that you want to help teens learn how to cook. So you hold a cooking class for a bunch of teenagers, but you realize that is not who you want to work with. That is great feedback from doing your leap. Another piece of learning you might obtain from doing your leap is that you find out what works and doesn't work if you do beta classes for your leap. It then takes the pressure off of you when you begin to offer the classes at a cost. You learned from your mistakes. You learned what you should include or take out of the classes in a way that you couldn't have discovered if, instead of leaping, you'd taken three months to design the class.

Time to Leap!

Now it is your turn to come up with a leap that you want to do. The leap should be able to be completed within the next two weeks, should be intimately linked with one of your passions, and should make you uncomfortable knowing that you have to go out there and stretch yourself. Keep it simple. Getting feedback and/or working with your target audience is key. You want to obtain feedback in a direct way from your leap. If you are writing a blog, then your feedback would be how many people made comments and shared your post. Who are the people that made the comments and shared it? How old were they? Were they male or female? If you are working at a dog-boarding business like Sally, your feedback could be from the owner and her thoughts after working with you for the weekend. Or even as indirect as the dogs. Did the dogs enjoy playing with you and having you around while they were being boarded? Gather as much information in your feedback as you can that will help you in moving forward once the leap is complete and you are ready to take action from there. So what do you want to do during those 20 seconds of insane courage? Go do it! Happy leaping!

Being directed down this new path, you are beginning to have an awareness that you didn't have previously. You can feel the yearning to move in the direction of filling that need. You are considering possible directions to head off in, further narrowing down your passions to go after. You are ready to take a leap, even before your plan is fully researched and perfected! A leap is a great way to figure out how you want to move forward and what you want to do so I know you will make me proud in taking that leap off the edge to begin soaring to see what will ignite you.

CHAPTER 8
INNER AND OUTER CRITIC

*"Life is found in the dance between your deepest
desire and your greatest fear."*

TONY ROBBINS

BEEP! BEEP! BEEP! The alarm bells are sounding! You
are stepping forward to change your life. BEEP! BEEP!
BEEP! A debilitating fear is rising within you. Your
breath is getting shallow. You are having a hard time swallowing.
Your chest is tightening up. What do you do now?

Hold on tight. The alarm bells are a normal part of the
process. When you begin to step forward to change your life,
a fear will arise in you. In this chapter we will be talking about
what these alarm bells are all about. They are rung by what I like
to call our inner critic. We will be talking about what exactly our
inner critic is and how to identify it in our lives. In playing bigger
and soaring, not everyone will be happy about you growing and

changing, and you will begin to notice outer critics coming out of the woodwork as well.

One of my favorite quotes is Susan Jeffers' "Feel the fear and do it anyway." You will be feeling many fears, and the key is to do it anyway. To push through it. When we begin to move outside of our comfort zone and out of the autopilot of everyday life, we will start hearing the voice of our inner critic. You may have also heard it referred to as the saboteur, the gremlin, or, more simply put, negative self-talk. You will recognize the voice of your inner critic because it goes for worst-case scenarios, telling you that you aren't good enough to be doing whatever you want to take on, or that it's an impossible task to do. Our inner critics are simply an expression of our fears.

Our inner critics are there to try to protect us by holding us back. The job of the inner critic is to try to keep you in the status quo and keep you playing small. It will twist, stretch, and distort the truth into a powerful argument to keep you from moving forward in doing your passion. I want to be honest with you: we all have inner critics. We all have fears, right? If you don't have one or more of them then I would love to meet you. Odds are, you hold a secret superpower and I would love to be able to eat or drink what you are having.

What we want to do is to know when it is the inner critic talking. Being able to identify when the inner critic is speaking and being aware of it when it is happening is the most important part of the process. Most of us do not even know that we have inner critics until they are externally pointed out to us. Without this awareness, we aren't able to take the steps to handle it and find ways to work through or around the inner critic. We will never be fully able to get rid of that inner critic voice inside of us, but over time, when we can identify it, we will know how to handle it better and it will cause less destruction in our minds.

Our brains are wired for fear. That is why we will never be able to get rid of the inner critic voice permanently. And we don't want to, because that part of our brain has saved our lives many times over. If we are getting ready to cross the street, lose our focus for one second, and a car darts out of nowhere in front of us, our automatic reaction is to jump out of the way. The part of the brain that is responsible for this automatic response to the fear and stress of getting hit by a car is the same part of the brain that is responsible for the fear and the inner critic. The only problem when this happens is that we lose the best part of our brain functioning. Our fear and stress center of our brain is online, and we lose the ability to think clearly. Our executive functions go offline, plus we are unable to feel the emotions that we need. That is why our inner critic sounds so irrational. Being able to identify when our inner critic is showing up will allow us to be able to bring our whole brain back online. We will be able to function and go full steam ahead. We won't be bulls in china shops. Bulls running around in china shops are never good. Imagine ourselves being directed by our inner critics and running wild in china shops. We need to save the glass! Luckily, even if we don't have a life coach or someone else in our lives making us aware, there are ways to identify when our inner critic is running the show.

Identifying When Your Inner Critic Is Present

The best thing for us to do is to be able to identify when our inner critic is showing up in a situation. Once we identify it, it loses its power. We are better able to handle it and know that it isn't our true inner voice talking. There are six ways to know whether it is our inner critic talking.

1. The inner critic sounds like a broken record. You will hear the same thoughts over and over again. For example, I'm not good enough to try out for that play. I will never get the part.

2. The voice will be negative, and often wants to tell you you're not good enough, stopping you in your tracks and from taking any sort of forward action. In thinking of the thought, would you say it to someone else? If the answer is no, then it is probably your inner critic speaking to you.

3. If you then beat yourself up for even thinking the thought that you had, it is probably your inner critic. After you sit there and criticize yourself, you have a moment of clarity and then beat yourself up for thinking it. That previous thought was your inner critic.

4. It gives you anxiety. It takes you into the fear and stress center of your brain where you can't think clearly therefore causing your adrenaline to go up.

5. One of my favorites is that your inner critic tricks you into thinking that it is looking out for your best interests, all the while trying to sabotage you. It makes it sound very realistic and that it will be the best outcome for you. For example, even when you're looking forward to going after a new job with more responsibilities and autonomy, your inner critic pops up to say that you'll look stupid to your family if you don't get that job, so you should just stay where you are now.

6. The voice inside of you may sound like your parents or a teacher that you had growing up who tried to keep you playing small. It is a twist on a role of the outer critic, but it has taken over as an inner critic.

Differentiating the Inner Critic and Your True Inner Voice

Now that you know the ways to identify your inner critic, I want to share with you a story about my client Mary. During one session, when she was speaking to me, I instantly knew that it was her inner critic talking. She was unaware that her inner critic had taken over her thoughts. When I pointed it out to her, it helped her begin to differentiate between her inner critic and her true inner voice speaking.

Mary said, "I've worked in a bakery for over 10 years, and I have always wanted to open a cupcake shop. I would love the opportunity to be my own boss and use my creativity to make the cupcakes that I enjoy making and be able to decorate them, but I don't know what I'm doing. I would have to gain more experience on learning to run a business because I have no idea how to even begin to do that, and I'll probably fail. I don't have the money to open a business, and like my father always said, I probably wouldn't succeed. I would be putting my family at financial risk, and I don't know if I want to take that chance. I just don't have what it takes to run a business."

Looking at this conversation with Mary, how do we know that it is her inner critic talking? Until I pointed it out to her, she thought it was her true inner voice thinking realistically about the situation. Instead, she took on the inner critic's narrative that she didn't know what she was doing and had no idea what it took to run a business. We can recognize it as being the inner critic voice because of it being a broken record. Just reading it as I wrote it out for this book made me anxious. She stated that she basically couldn't do it. Her tone was very negative, and was stopping her from taking any sort of forward action. Her inner critic tricked her by making her think that even though she wanted the opportunity to become her own boss and use her creativity, it was protecting her from doing it because she didn't know what she was doing. There was critique in the statement instead of a loving and caring voice. Lastly, she had the voice of her father in her head keeping her playing small and making her feel that she couldn't do it. That stopped her right in her tracks instead of helping her figure out a way to do her passion and open a cupcake shop.

How would this conversation have gone differently if Mary's inner critic hadn't taken over her, and her true inner voice had spoken instead? Let's take a look at how different it might be:

"I've worked in a bakery for over 10 years, and I have always wanted to open a cupcake shop. I would love the opportunity to be my own boss and to use my creativity to make the cupcakes that I enjoy making and be able to decorate them, but I don't have what I need right now. I wonder how I could find out what is needed. I will ask the bakery owner if he will meet with me to ask him how he started his business to learn more about that this week. That feels doable and exciting. I am really committed to being able to support my family financially. I wonder how I would be able to do my business while maintaining the support. That is important to me and I don't want to give up my dream."

This line of conversation is more rational than the first one. She is interested in gaining more information and not focusing on the negative and not being able to do it. The second way of thinking gets her into forward action toward attaining her dream. During Mary's and my time working together, she was able to gain more awareness of when her inner critic was showing up in her life. She realized that her inner critic could show up in many facets of her life, not just in her professional work.

Personifying Your Inner Critic

That is what you want to do for yourself when you notice your inner critic peeking its head out. As you are moving forward and pushing yourself towards your passion and out of your comfort zone, your inner critic is going to come out in full force, and I want to help you recognize when and how it shows up. Recognizing your inner critic and being aware of it when you are speaking will reduce the power that it has over you. You are not the person the inner critic is speaking of. The best thing that you can do is to recognize it when it shows up, name it, and separate it from you. We want to have the inner critic as more of the background music that's playing instead of the music that is jamming on the radio. We don't want it to direct our choices. The better we can get at recognizing the inner critic, the less frequent and quieter the inner critic will become in our lives.

One of the things that we can do once we identify the inner critic to help separate it from ourselves and see that it is not our true inner voice is personifying it by getting to know your inner critic. This is a tool that I learned at the Coaches Training Institute. Thinking about that negative self-talk you hear in your head, what is your inner critic saying to you? What is its story? What are some of the things that your inner critic says to you most frequently?

How would you describe your inner critic? Let's personify your inner critic by giving it a name and bringing it to life like a character. Our inner critics are separate from us, and this gives you the opportunity to see the inner critic come to life outside of you. Bring to mind things that your inner critic says to you. When the inner critic is talking, do you notice that it is a female or a male voice? Is it an older or younger voice? Now let's imagine your inner critic as a person. What would the person look like? Is it a fictional character that you make up or is it a person or figure from a movie, book, politics, etc.? Is it a real-life person that you know? If it is someone close to you, give it a different name so it will take on a life of its own. Maybe your inner critic character is an old high school teacher or an old boss?

To bring your inner critic to life, what does he or she wear? Where does your inner critic live? What does your critic eat and do in its spare time? Now come up with a name for your inner critic and begin to call it by name when you see it pop up in your life.

My Inner Critic Personified

I want to share with you my first experience of personifying my inner critic. I named my inner critic Mr. Box Restrictor, and I drew a picture of him to help bring him to life. He looked like one of those blockheads from the show *Gumby*. He was red with a rubber body and had a block for a head.

Mr. Box Restrictor loves living within the box. He is always smiling and pretending to be happy. He is scamming me though by the words he says to me to keep me playing inside of my box and comfort zone. He drives a Cadillac Escalade and lives in Beverly Hills. For breakfast, he loves having his morning tea and cherries. Not really sure where the cherries came from, but that is what I had written that he loves to eat.

Personifying my inner critic helped me to notice that my inner critic is not me. It is just a voice that I have inside of myself. In doing this, it helped me to take my inner critic less seriously. I knew he would pop back up, but next time I would be able to recognize when he is there. Learning to become aware of your inner critic is key to being able to manage it and move past it. You want to know what the motivations of your inner critic are because that is why they keep showing up.

Recognizing Outer Critics

Outer critics are everywhere, and they each have their own motivations for being in our way. The outer critics are people who try to bring you down and hold you back from doing your passions. The biggest thing you need to understand with outer critics is that the majority of the time, they are not maliciously trying to hold you back. Your outer critics are not even aware that they are doing that to you.

Your outer critics are most likely the people that are closest to you: your spouse, your mother, your father, your family and friends. If you had to identify any outer critics that you have in your life right now, who would they be? People are afraid of change and how it will change the status quo, so they project their fear (and the voices of their own inner critics) onto you through their negativity. They might tell you that you aren't good enough to do "that," or ask you who are you to take the chance to do "that" when they are stuck at their job. They could use financial reasons to try to hold you back. Whatever they are able to use as leverage is game-on for them. They could use your past against you. You never committed to anything in your life, so what makes you think you will start now with this new journey or adventure?

When I was starting out in my coaching business, I was really motivated and determined. I got my coaching certification and started my own business. I was an entrepreneur. There was a piece of me that had always wanted to have my own business growing up, to be just like my father since he has his own business.

I was excited to be able to talk to him about my business and to learn things from him. Our family had gone on vacation to Deep Creek Lake in Maryland. It was nighttime and there were five of us sitting outside enjoying the fresh air and the clear sky with the stars shining brightly down on us. We were all sitting cozily around a bonfire and talking. I don't get to see my family too much since I live in a different state, so I was excited by the opportunity to see them and talk to them.

My dad and my brother-in-law were talking about their businesses, and I thought it would be the perfect opportunity to tell my dad about my coaching and how it was going. I had it all perfectly set in my mind, asking him questions on how he markets and what suggestions he had for me to get out there to get people. I wanted to get tips from him and hear lessons learned from the over 30 years of him owning his own business. It didn't go as planned. Every time I brought up my coaching, he ignored me. He changed the subject with each sentence I said. It was as if he was telling me that he knew I would fail and that I should quit wasting my time and go back to doing accounting like he told me to go do all those years ago when I went into college. It was a huge disappointment to me.

My dad was one of my outer critics, but I didn't recognize him as such until that day. It had me extremely upset, and after him changing the subject and not even acknowledging what I was doing, I reacted. I told him that I was trying to tell him about my business and what I was doing, and he changed the subject every time. That was the day that I told my dad where to go in no uncertain terms, and I walked away from that beautiful night sky and bonfire. Oh yes, I did that. I took back my power that day. I still talk to my dad and everything is fine, but I don't recall talking to him about anything to do with my coaching business or anything work-related since that day.

We have a choice when we are faced with our outer critics. We can let them stomp on our dreams and passions and stop us from becoming who we are created to be, or we can sidestep them and not let them put out our fires. I chose to not let my dad put out my fire. We can't change another person to make them fit into who we want them to be in our lives. But we do have the power to change ourselves. I hope that by being able to recognize your inner critics and outer critics and managing them when they present themselves to you, you can continue to move forward in your journey to living out your passion and soaring in your life.

CHAPTER 9
NEW FOUNDATION TO BUILD

"Consider a tree for a moment. As beautiful as trees are to look at, we don't see what goes on underground as they grow roots. Trees must develop deep roots in order to grow strong and produce their beauty. But we don't see the roots. We just see and enjoy the beauty. In much the same way, what goes on inside of us is like the roots of a tree."

JOYCE MEYER

Y ou planted little seedlings in the ground while you were doing your leap. The seedlings started to grow and take root as you started on your new path. In this chapter, we will be focusing on the story that you want to tell now in your life moving forward. You will be making a commitment to this new journey and building a foundation from which to grow.

When starting anew, it is best to take the time up front and begin to build a strong foundation. The time you take now to build it out will help later on when your inner and outer critics come up with obstacles to deter you from moving forward and try to knock you off your path. When I think of building a strong foundation, my mind goes to thinking about trees. When a tree is growing, it needs to have strong roots – when the tree is still a sapling, the wind can tumble it over if the roots aren't strong enough.

The roots of a tree grow down and out. They will grow around objects that are in their way. The roots are very sturdy. Having a steady base allows the tree to grow freely. The tree is free to build out its branches on which leaves can bloom. It builds a luscious tree filled with leaves. The tree would not be able to flourish without the strong roots. The farther the reach of those roots, the more water and nutrients the tree is able to bring in and the more oxygen the tree will be able to give off.

Creating a New Intention

Just like the tree, I want you to be able to start on this new journey growing out your roots so you will have a strong base to begin with. The seeds have already been planted and the roots are beginning to grow from completing your leap. The next thing for you to do in growing this strong base and expanding your roots is make a commitment to move forward. This is similar to the Creating an Intention exercise that we did in Step 1. Now that you are in a different space and have narrowed your direction after completing your leap, you may feel it is time to create a new, more focused intention for moving forward. As I mentioned in Step 1, I believe that intentions are the starting point to get our mind, body, spirit, and the universe in line with each other. If we don't put out there what we want, then the chance of it coming into realization diminishes. I believe that when we set intentions, we use our time and energy more wisely, putting them toward what we are wanting.

Having done your leap and planted the seedlings for your tree, you are ready now to move on in building your foundation. This will help ensure the tree has strong roots as you grow. To create this new intention, I would love for you to go to a quiet place when you are writing it. Grab a notebook and a pen and write it down. I want you to take about five minutes and just marinate on the question: *What is your intention for the passion calling you?* This will probably be more of a concrete answer than the one you set in Step 1.

After you write your intention down, take a moment to close your eyes and embody the new presence being created. You are at a new place in this process, so I want you to think of the person that you want to become as a result. Imagine your intention that you just set in place and focus your thoughts on bringing it into fruition. Breathe in the intention as you breathe five deep breaths. Allow it to fill each crevice in your body and all of the spaces. What does it feel like to have this intention created in you? As you are breathing out, imagine breathing out more of the old, unfulfilled pieces of you. You might be noticing you are able to breathe out more pieces of it than you did the first time, or maybe not. Don't judge it. Just notice what is happening in your body. Now, if it feels right, take a few notes of what is going on in your body and in your mind. What thoughts are you having right now?

Susan's New Intention

When my client Susan landed at this step in her journey she thought it was a good time to get re-centered with where she was in her journey and to set a new intention. This would help her to realign herself with the steps she now wanted to take after seeing her path moving forward as a result of doing her leap. Susan was working as a business analyst, and wasn't fulfilled by it. She went through the exercises of identifying her passions and doing a leap to see where it landed with her in wanting to advance in her journey. For her leap, she created a fashion blog. That is where her passion was taking her. She started planting the seedlings for her tree to take root in doing her leap. The leap ignited a spark inside of her, and she was ready to move forward. She was ready to set the new intention that was more focused. Her new intention was to bring her love for fashion out into the world by helping others put together fashionable outfits. Notice that her intention was more centered on the avenue she wanted to get into without being very specific. Specificity would limit the branches that may grow from putting herself out into the fashion world.

Saying Yes to Moving Forward

Now it is time to make a commitment. A commitment to sticking with and moving forward in realizing your passion. I want you to say *yes* to moving forward, building a foundation, and growing strong roots to be able to have your tree grow and flourish. What do you want to commit to going forward? It might be committing to take the steps to doing your passion. Maybe it also includes committing to not letting your inner and outer critics stop you from realizing your passion. Susan said yes to moving forward and committed to continuing to write her fashion blog and working on getting clients to help them expand their wardrobes. In thinking about making a commitment, ask yourself: What am I trying to achieve and how would I go after it? What is my goal?

You created a new intention and made a commitment to moving forward in the pursuit of your passion, now what is the truth you want to empower? Maybe it is your ability to be brave and courageous in taking the steps that you need in order to be fulfilled. Not only are you stepping into your commitment to move forward, you are stepping into a new being that was birthed. Stepping into this new being is part of growing strong roots. The person you were at the beginning of this journey is not the same person that you are right now. You have opened your awareness and stepped outside of your comfort zone. I love the quote from Albert Einstein that says, "The mind that opens to a new idea never returns to its original size." With this new awareness of yourself and the role you are to play in the world, it will be hard to return to what you were doing before, living with that hole in your heart and feeling unfulfilled.

Being with Your People

Being around like-minded individuals and others that have the energy that you want to exude is a great way to get you grounded and rooted in your new existence. I call it "being with your people." It will help you to be in the frame of mind to continue moving forward toward your passion and help reflect the person that you want to be. They will help remind you of your strength and power when you get scared or uncertain and don't yet see them for yourself.

When I was going through the process of becoming a life coach, I surrounded myself with other coaches. Besides being in the coaching classes with them, I would set aside time to be around them, whether it was asking for advice on what works for them or spending my free time with them to enjoy their company. The people that are like-minded and have the energy you want usually carry that energy around them all the time, not just during business hours. I found this to be key in growing and expanding myself. To this day, I still take the time to hang out or have lunch with other coaches. I will set up work dates with other coaches as well. The energy and camaraderie is important to me in continuing on this journey. You will find what works for you and enjoy picking the brains of other like-minded individuals. We have so much to learn from each other. Why not take advantage of it when we can?

Identifying Allies in Your Life

In the last chapter, you learned to tame your inner and outer critics. That will be a continuous battle throughout your journey in moving forward. One way to combat those critics is by identifying allies in your life right now. These are the people who believe in you and believe you are meant to do something greater. When you are feeling uncertain about your passion or your path, these are the people who will hold that mirror in front of you and show you your strength, proof that you can do it. These allies can be family members, friends, colleagues, mentors, or a life coach. Identify at least one or two allies to contact to inform them of your passion and commitment in moving forward, so they will be available to support you along the way. Think about what sort of support you want to receive from them. Do you want a call or an email to see how you are doing, or to have them on speed dial when your inner critic is getting the best of you? You can reach out to them for positive words to get you going on the right track again. It's important to have allies or cheerleaders in your corner as you are going into uncharted territory. It makes the journey feel not so hard.

At the start of any new journey, I find it is vital to build a strong foundation so when the tougher times come, our foundation will stay intact. Just like a tree that has its roots growing down and outwards, getting water and resources to keep the tree strong, build your foundation by setting new intentions to move forward and at each platform along the way to ensure you are in alignment. Making a commitment to yourself for the journey ahead allows you to know that you are firmly planting yourself in the ground.

To help you maintain that strong foundation, it is best to have other like-minded energetic beings and allies around you. This helps you when you are growing and keeps you on track so your growth doesn't get hindered by outside or inside influences. You want to arm yourself with the best possible support team so you can move toward fulfillment and set yourself up for success.

CHAPTER 10
GETTING INTO ACTION

"And the day came when the risk to remain tight in a bud was more painful than the risk it took to blossom."

ANAIS NIN

You started building your foundation by expanding your roots in the last chapter. In this next step, we'll look to a simple toy, Jack-in-the-Box, for motivation. We will talk about what's next in your journey and start taking small steps to get you started on your way to soaring in your life. You will begin to take the lead in your life.

Wisdom from the Jack-in-the-Box

You remember Jack-in-the-Box, right? It was a box that had a crank on the outside. When you turned the crank, it played the melody of "Pop Goes the Weasel." At the end of the tune, the lid popped open and a clown sprang out of the box. The Jack-in-the-Box's origin traces back to the 13th century. The wisdom that Jack has soaked in over the years is infinite.

I have a theory for Jack being around for so many centuries. Jack is here to guide you to break through your limited, stuck-in-your-box mindset and to help you spring out into action. When you began on this journey, it was similar to you being stuck in your box like Jack. Feeling unfulfilled and having that hole inside of you. Playing small in your life. You would wake up every day, go to your day-to-day 40-hours-a-week job, come home, make dinner, watch television, then crash. This was a continuous cycle. You were trying to find a you in that cycle. You hated it, but didn't have the energy or the want to take the risk of shifting the stability of the already cracked retaining wall. I bet you started to really question who that person in the box is. Is it really me? Then you found this book. Thank goodness.

You have gone through the steps to make it to this point in your journey. Let's take a look at the magic Jack brings and how he can help spring you forward to take action from here. Come with me to show you the magic of Jack! Let's get Jack-Out-of-the-Box. Imagine yourself as Jack right now in his box and moving to pop out of the box and spring into action.

When you are in the box it's dark in there. You can't see anything, and you don't know which way is up. That is how you felt before starting this process. I invite you to get present in the now. Be calm and focused as you look around. Suddenly you see a crack of light coming from the worn edge of one of the corners of your box.

You saw the crack of light. You listed your passions and did the leap to see what landed for you. Where did the crack come from? You looked there at least a 100 times before. What's different this time? What changed after your leap? You? You started to begin to build your foundation to move forward, so you go up to the opening. Can you see what is out there?

What is out there? Is the crack big enough to see out? It might be best to stay in the box; it's comfortable, it's known, it's safe. *But* what if you take the chance and pop out of your box? There are people laughing and skipping and carrying on with joy. Enjoying what they do for a living and feeling fulfilled. Take a chance on peeking your head out of the crack to breathe in the light.

We need to understand that we can choose. You have the ability to make a conscious decision based on what feels right inside, this is why you first have to go through the prior six steps to become aware that you have a choice. Each choice will not be easy, and you may encounter many obstacles on the way. If you don't continue forward, what are you giving up by not choosing and letting it or another person choose for you?

You chose to take the chance and pop out of your box by doing this journey. Now what? Your goal isn't accomplished yet. It is just starting. Now is the time to firmly stand in your commitment of creating the change you want to see in yourself! Are you ready?

Get Jack-Out-of-the-Box! We use phrases like "think outside the box" and "getting outside your comfort zone" to help others expand their minds. If we stay inside the Jack-in-the-

Box, there is no room in our lives for change and greatness. I call upon you to take yourself out of the box! Substitute *your* name for Jack's. Get *Melissa-Out-of-the-Box!* It feels momentous out here springing back and forth with my hands out, welcoming in the world. I may not be well-equipped yet, but I am committed to continue springing around and dodging all obstacles that come my way on the path to a more fulfilling, passionate life. I welcome you to do the same. The springing starts by exploring what is next in your journey.

Once you are out, it is a struggle for yourself and others to put you back in the box. This is one of the blessings that Mr. Jack-in-the-Box gives to you. Even though you are able to shove Jack back in his box, you aren't wired the same way. You discovered a new path. It is time to take action by springing out of your box and taking forward action toward the goals that you set for yourself.

Create a List of Next Steps

Now you get to decide what is next. You don't want to go back inside of your box like we can do with Jack. It is time to take the lead in your life. This is the tipping point. The inner critic voices are probably getting louder. Using the ways to identify the voices will help silence them. When looking over the next year, you need to decide: What's your time frame for making this change in your life? How long do you want to give yourself to attain this goal?

Once this is established, then you can begin to make a list of the steps needed to get to this goal. When you are thinking of a list of steps to take to get to your goal of doing your passion, start small. Using a combination of small steps will set you up for success. Going straight from working at a job at which you are unfulfilled to quitting and unemployment isn't the best way to jump-start your new passion. This might work from some people, but we want to maximize your odds of success. Therefore, if you were to write down a list of five steps that you can begin to start taking today to get you closer to where you want to be, what would they be? Think baby steps when you are making this list. You want to go from A to B to C to D and so forth. You do not want to skip from B to H. This will slow your progress and bring more stress to your life. Even when you proceed sequentially, you may learn along the way that you skipped from A to E and have to go back to fill in the B, C, and D.

When I was starting to take action after I determined that I wanted to become a life coach, the first five steps I established were: 1) talk to other coaches that I knew to learn where they got certified and if they believed a certification was necessary, 2) research coaching certification programs to find which institute would be the best fit for me if I were going to continue forward in getting my certification, 3) reach out to a couple of the institutes to speak to a representative and learn more about the companies, 4) review all of my options that I had in front of me for life coaching, and 5) make a decision about if I wanted to get certified and which certification program I would sign up for.

When Molly started working with me, she felt just like the Jack-in-the-Box. She could see the cracks of light from inside the box and her springs were coiled with tension knowing that she was meant to do something greater in her life, but she didn't know the way out. She was stuck in her thinking of what she wanted to do next, but she didn't want to stay where she was currently working for an advertising agency. "I don't even like marketing," she told me. "I change the channel every time I see a commercial on television, that's how much I hate it. I dread going into work every day."

She discovered that a pivotal point in her life was when her sister had a premature baby and had to be in the NICU for months. "Ever since I had to go through seeing my niece in the hospital for those couple months after she was born and how the nurses treated the babies and cared for them as they were their own, I had it in the back of my mind that I would want to do that someday," she said. "I just always pushed it off that I would do it when I had more money or time to go back to school."

After Molly completed her leap of going back to the hospital where her niece was born to see the NICU and to sit down with three of the nurses to speak with them about their experiences and set a new intention going forward, it was time for her to spring into action. I asked her, "Now that you know that you want to move forward in becoming a nurse in the NICU, what would be the next steps to take to make this happen? I want you to succeed in doing this, so we want to take it slow, breaking it down into baby steps. This will allow yourself to set goals that will take you from A to Z, not skipping any steps in the middle.

If you were to start today, what would be the first thing that you would do to get started on that path?"

"Well, I already talked to some of the nurses at the hospital where my niece was during my leap so I got their opinion on some good universities to go to," Molly said. "I guess I would first take the time to do some research online of universities around my area that offer nursing. I just realized that I will probably also have to take more undergraduate classes because I didn't have to take a lot of science classes when I majored in marketing." "That's great," I replied. "You already stated two steps that you need to take in moving forward. What would be three more steps that you could note right now to get you started?"

Molly paused for a minute, thinking about the steps that she would need. "Ok, so if I start doing research of universities that offer nursing, then see what classes I need to take for my undergraduate degree, I would need to talk to two or three representatives at the colleges that I am looking to go to for more information. Then I would need to get my transcripts from my university to give to the representative so see what courses I need to take. The fifth thing would probably be finding out if I have enough time to apply and get started in the fall semester. I might be cutting it close."

Add a Deadline Date

After you come up with your list of five things to do next to move forward in your journey, it's time to put a deadline date on when you want to accomplish these items. When we put a date on it as to when you want to get it accomplished, it makes it more tangible. It helps to keep our mind focused and puts more accountability on us. What will you do if you miss your deadline?

My list with my deadlines would've looked something like this if I'd started my journey on May 1st:

1. Talk to other coaches – May 4th

2. Research coaching certification programs – May 7th

3. Contact multiple coaching programs – May 14th

4. Review my options – May 18th

5. Make a decision – May 21st

With the dates listed, your mind automatically starts sorting out the information and how to begin to go about accomplishing those tasks. Know who you need to contact by what date.

Getting an Accountability Partner

An added layer to help keep you on track in this process is having an accountability partner. This could be a life coach or a friend. An accountability partner is someone who knows what you are planning to do and helps you stick to your goals. They help ensure you are successful at what you are setting out to do. Life gets in our way when we are making plans, especially big plans. Circumstances as well as both inner and outer critics will try to throw you off track. Having an accountability partner is a great way to keep you on your way to being successful at achieving your dreams.

Resources Already At Your Fingertips

To get started in taking your actions, what resources do you already have available to you that enable you to get started immediately? What connections do you have that will help educate you or move you closer toward your goals? What skills or information do you have inside that will also be of service to you in your new path? Resources might also include money available that might be needed, depending on the passion you are going after.

The Jack-in-the-Box is a great example of showing us how to go from being stuck in our boxes to coming out of the box and springing forward into action. In looking at what is next in the process, it is best to begin by creating a list of small steps to take to set yourself up for success. Adding deadlines to the steps will help keep your focus in moving forward. I suggest getting an accountability partner to be by your side through this process to help keep you on track and provide the motivation along the way. Take advantage of resources that you already have in your life and in yourself to help you get started immediately on your journey. The hard work you put in the journey is worth it. Start today and take action forward.

CHAPTER 11
CONCLUSION

"Do you have the courage? Do you have the courage to bring forth this work? The treasures that are hidden inside you are hoping you will say yes."

ELIZABETH GILBERT, *Big Magic*

Do you remember where the status of your mind was at the outset of this journey? You woke up every day with that hole in your heart. You looked at yourself in the mirror every morning and just felt the hole growing deeper and deeper as the days went on. You went into work feeling like a fraud. You operated on auto-pilot. The work got completed, but no love went into the work. You felt unfulfilled and were ready to make a lasting change.

Your S.O.A.R.I.N.G. process began by imagining a bigger space in the world for you to fill. You created an intention and put it out in the universe, aligning your mind, body, and soul for the journey. You took the time to see what you already had inside of you by writing I Am statements. A seed was being planted.

You started to realize the parts of you that you wanted to highlight to ignite the fire within. You accomplished this by looking at pivotal moments that you had in life that charted your course up to this point, then taking a look at what drives you. You explored yourself through the two inner journey visualizations of speaking in front of a crowd for 30 seconds to change the lives of those you were speaking to and to write a message on a billboard for everyone that drove by to see. You brought to mind three of your top values in life and decided whether those values were being honored in your life. Then you took the time to take inventory of what you were passionate about in life.

You began to have a relationship with your passion, getting to know it like you would a friend. You took a look at an area of quiet desperation in your life and what you would do if you weren't afraid. You used the powerful tool of reframing to look differently at limiting old beliefs that held you back. To move forward in a more resourceful way, you created permission slips for places in your life where you were holding yourself back. Lastly, you took yourself through a visualization of walking through the tunnel of trees and into the fog, with the fog clearing at the end of the tunnel. You received a gift from the universe at the stump of a tree in front of you on the path.

A new direction in your path began, and with this new awareness came the responsibility to fill the need that you were feeling inside. You wrote down targets that you wanted to attain to further narrow down your passions. Using your 20 seconds of insane courage, you did a leap within one to two weeks and obtained feedback.

The alarm bells were sounding with fears rising inside of you. You learned to recognize inner and outer critics and how to handle them. You learned ways to identify and personify your inner critic to defuse its power. You saw the outer critics in your life, and that their fear is more about them than it is about you.

Next, you made a commitment to yourself on your new journey by beginning to build a foundation. Building a foundation is like a tree having good and strong roots to grow and flourish. You created a new intention going forward and made a commitment to the process of making your passion a reality. You learned that it is to your advantage to surround yourself with allies, people that embody what you want to bring into your life.

You took the lead in this new creation of yourself that you are now aware of and started to take action. Jack-in-the-Box enlightened you on his perspective from being in his box to popping out to spring into action. You identified small steps to help you move forward and put deadlines on them to get you into action immediately. Having an accountability partner in this process will increase the chance of you succeeding in your journey. Checking resources that you already have available to you will also help you in being able to move forward as soon as possible.

As you are moving through your journey, remember to take time to celebrate along the way. With each milestone that you hit or deadline that you accomplish, do something to celebrate, whether it's just a pat on the back, a spa day, or a nice dinner out. Celebrating along the way helps make the journey more enjoyable, and you appreciate yourself more for the work you are putting into it.

I want to share with you a poem that I wrote in February 2016. This is a poem that I wrote one evening when I couldn't sleep and I was thinking about where I was in my own process. To dare myself to push forward and continue to soar in my life. My wish for you is to never settle and always dare yourself to dream bigger. To want more from your life because we only have this one life to live.

I DARE YOU

I dare you to do that one thing you've always wanted to do.

I dare you to stretch the limits of your comfort zone.

I dare you to move past what has been stopping you.

I dare you to dream bigger than you are already.

I dare you to shout out your insecurities.

I dare you to be happy.

I dare you to know what success feels like.

I dare you to love that one person a little bit more.

I dare you to let that person love you a little bit more.

I dare you to forgive someone that did you wrong.

I dare you to stop making excuses for why you can't do something.

I dare you to be thankful for each day you wake up alive.

I dare you to say yes.

I dare you to say no.

I dare you to love yourself.

I dare you!

Now go out there and live your life. Don't take life for granted. I was given a second chance to live my life, and I don't want to waste a second of it. I truly believe that I was hit in the head for you! My life stopped for a while so you can learn how to begin yours. I have begun mine, and I want to see you do the same. We were all meant for something greater. We were meant to wake up each day and make a difference in other people's lives. To be fulfilled in what we do and to be able to take that step off the edge to soar in our lives. I want to see you go further than you ever thought you could go. I dare you!

I dare you to live wholeheartedly, fulfilled and without regrets. Check your heart, then change your mind. Use your wings to soar. You never know where you will land.

ACKNOWLEDGMENTS

I dedicated my book to all survivors. Over the course of my life, I have met so many strong survivors of all types. Each one of you has given me the courage to continue forward on my journey. After my brain injury, I felt alone and isolated. Finding other brain injury survivors that understood what I was going through changed the course of my recovery. I would not be in the place I am today without your support. Thank you! And a big thank you to the Trauma Survivors Network. The support groups and the volunteering to visit brain injury patients in the hospital truly fills my soul every time I go. It has inspired me to get my message out to help change the lives of as many people as my reach can touch.

To my mother, Carol: the strength and love you have is an incredible example to me that I have learned to have in my life. You have supported me and been there during my trying times. I am proud to be your daughter. You told us we can do anything we want in life and I believed you. So here I am. Thank you for being a rock in my life.

To my father, Nick: I inherited your stubbornness and drive to succeed in business. Thank you for your love and support in life. It doesn't go unnoticed.

To my sisters, Rachel and Valerie: I can always feel your love and support even though physically I am not nearby. Your friendships mean the world to me, and I am lucky to have the best sisters anyone could ask for in life.

To my seven nieces and nephews, Sierra, Chloe, Hunter, Riley, Brayden, David and Mia: Your love and laughter light up my life. You make my world manageable and more fulfilled.

To my brother and in-laws, Nicky, Christie, Mike, and Shawn: Thank you for the support that you give me and all of the fun times that we have together as a family.

To my grandma, Eileen: I can always feel your love across the miles. You make me feel very loved. I love when I get to see your smile and be in your presence. Your toughness rubbed off to help me get through my tough times and to never roll over in life.

To one of my closest friends, Stacy Trice: You have been a pillar for me for almost 20 years now. We have shared so many adventures together. You have always been there for me, providing me advice and guidance along the way, but most importantly friendship. Your friendship and your love that you give are hard to find and I'm lucky to be blessed with you in my life.

To my writing and working buddy, Danielle Karst: I would not have made it through the writing process as smoothly if it weren't for our writing dates. You provided me with enough distraction to keep me sane. I thank you for your company and your friendship.

To my kitty, Phoebus: You have been my buddy through all of this. You have seen the good and bad parts of me and were by my side since my brain injury happened. The love and energy that you give and provide to me is so magnificent. I would not have made it this far in my journey without you there.

To my book coach, Angela Lauria: Thank you for seeing the message and movement that needs to be spread to the world through me. The energy and fierceness you exude is being soaked in by everyone you meet. Thank you for the invaluable insight along the journey and deep care that you show. It is greatly appreciated.

To Maggie McReynolds: Thank you for helping to make this book even more amazing. You have a gift, and I am thankful that you were part of my book publishing process.

To the Morgan James Publishing team: Special thanks to David Hancock, CEO & Founder for believing in me and my message. To my Author Relations Manager, Megan Malone, thanks for making the process seamless and easy. Many more thanks to everyone else, but especially Jim Howard, Bethany Marshall, and Nickcole Watkins.

To the person that hit me in the head with the softball: Even though you denied doing it years later, I thank you for not having the awareness to not throw the ball to me when there was no play. I would not be in the place I am today without your carelessness.

ABOUT THE AUTHOR

Melissa S. Morrison is a recovering accountant and a brain injury thriver who has found her passion as a life coach and an author. She specializes in working with people who want to stretch the edges of their comfort zone by transforming and taking the lead in their lives. As a traumatic brain injury survivor, she understands what it means to personally transform.

Melissa obtained her coaching certification from the Coaches Training Institute as a Co-Active Professional Coach. She is a Certified Neurosculpting® Facilitator from the Neurosculpting® Institute, aimed at improving lives using neuroscience through education of overall brain health and re-wiring old stories through meditation.

Her career background in leadership and business in auditing, consulting, and fraud creates a unique viewpoint as a life coach. As a Certified Fraud Examiner, she is equipped with the tools to recognize and eliminate the personal fraud we all hide behind.

Melissa currently resides in McLean, VA with her tuxedo-colored cat. She loves spending time with her family and enjoys running, cooking, and spending time outdoors in nature.

Contact:

Melissa@melissasmorrison.com

THANK YOU

Thanks for reading *Unstick Your Stuck*. The fact that you've gotten to this point in the book tells me that you're ready. You are ready to stop feeling unfilled and start soaring.

I'm excited to get you moving forward on your path to ensure that you break free from the brain patterns that aren't supporting you anymore. To get you started, I'm giving you a free audio class called *Could Neuroscience Explain Why You're Stuck?* It will help you understand why your brain is keeping you stuck in unfulfillment and give you tips to create new neural pathways in the brain to break free and create lasting change in your life.

You can download the audio class by going to my website, http://www.MelissaSMorrison.com/FreeClass.

Morgan James
Speakers Group

We connect Morgan James published
authors with live and online events
and audiences who will benefit
from their expertise.

Morgan James makes all of our titles available
through the Library for All Charity Organization.

www.LibraryForAll.org

Printed in the USA
CPSIA information can be obtained
at www.ICGtesting.com
JSHW082353140824
68134JS00020B/2059